1 JOHN

THE TEST OF FAITH

AT A GLANCE

Serendipity House / P.O. Box 1012 / Littleton, CO 80160

TOLL FREE 1-800-525-9563 / www.serendipityhouse.com

98 99 00 01 / **301 series • CHG** / 4 3 2 1

PROJECT ENGINEER:
Lyman Coleman

WRITING TEAM:
Richard Peace, Lyman Coleman, Andrew Sloan, Cathy Tardif

PRODUCTION TEAM:
Christopher Werner, Sharon Penington, Erika Tiepel

COVER PHOTO:
© 1998 J. Vanuga / Westlight

CORE VALUES

Community:	The purpose of this curriculum is to build community within the body of believers around Jesus Christ.
Group Process:	To build community, the curriculum must be designed to take a group through a step-by-step process of sharing your story with one another.
Interactive Bible Study:	To share your "story," the approach to Scripture in the curriculum needs to be open-ended and right brain—to "level the playing field" and encourage everyone to share.
Developmental Stages:	To provide a healthy program in the life cycle of a group, the curriculum needs to offer courses on three levels of commitment: (1) Beginner Stage—low-level entry, high structure, to level the playing field; (2) Growth Stage—deeper Bible study, flexible structure, to encourage group accountability; (3) Discipleship Stage—in-depth Bible study, open structure, to move the group into high gear.
Target Audiences:	To build community throughout the culture of the church, the curriculum needs to be flexible, adaptable and transferable into the structure of the average church.

ACKNOWLEDGMENTS

To Zondervan Bible Publishers
for permission to use
the NIV text,
The Holy Bible, New International Bible Society.
© 1973, 1978, 1984 by International Bible Society.
Used by permission of Zondervan Bible Publishers.

WELCOME TO THE SERENDIPITY 301 DEPTH BIBLE STUDY SERIES

You are about to embark on an adventure into the powerful experience of depth Bible Study. The Serendipity 301 series combines three basic elements to produce a life-changing and group-changing course.

First, you will be challenged and enriched by the personal Bible Study that begins each unit. You will have the opportunity to dig into Scripture both for understanding and personal reflection. Although some groups may choose to do this section together at their meeting, doing it beforehand will greatly add to the experience of the course.

Second, you will benefit from the group sessions. Wonderful things happen when a small group of people get together and share their lives around the Word of God. Not only will you have a chance to take your personal study to a deeper level, you will have an opportunity to share on a deep level what's happening in your life and receive the encouragement and prayer support of your group.

Third, the 301 courses provide the stimulus and tools for your group to take steps toward fulfilling your group mission. Whether or not your group has gone through the preparation of a Serendipity 101 and 201 course, you can profit from this mission emphasis. The 32-page center section of this book will guide you through this process. And questions in the closing section of the group agenda will prompt your group to act upon the mission challenge to "give birth" to a new small group.

Put these three components together, and you have a journey in Christian discipleship well worth the effort. Enjoy God's Word! Enjoy genuine Christian community! Enjoy dreaming about your mission!

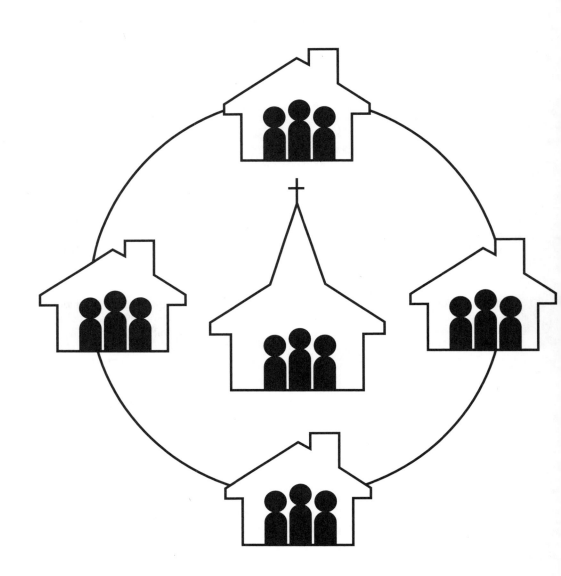

QUESTIONS & ANSWERS

STAGE

1. *What stage in the life cycle of a small group is this course designed for?*

Turn to the first page of the center section of this book. There you will see that this 301 course is designed for the third stage of a small group. In the Serendipity "Game Plan" for the multiplication of small groups, your group is in the Release Stage.

GOALS

2. *What are the goals of a 301 study course?*

As shown on the second page of the center section (page M2), the focus in this third stage is heavy on Bible Study and Mission.

BIBLE STUDY

301

3. *What is the approach to Bible Study in this course?*

This course involves two types of Bible Study. The "homework" assignment fosters growth in personal Bible study skills and in personal spiritual growth. The group study gives everyone a chance to share their learning and together take it to a deeper level.

SELF STUDY

4. *What does the homework involve?*

There are three parts to each assignment: (1) READ—to get the "bird's-eye view" of the passage and record your first impressions; (2) SEARCH—to get the "worm's-eye view" by digging into the passage verse-by-verse with specific questions; and (3) APPLY—to ask yourself, after studying the passage, "What am I going to do about it?"

THREE-STAGE LIFE CYCLE OF A GROUP

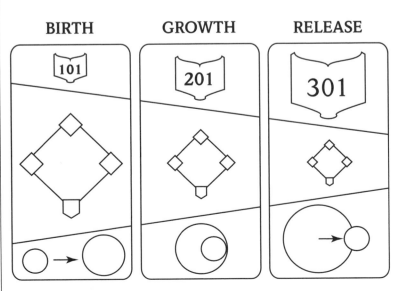

BIRTH   GROWTH   RELEASE

5

BIBLE KNOWLEDGE

5. *What if you don't know very much about the Bible?*

No problem. The homework assignment is designed to lead you step-by-step in your study. And there are study notes in each unit to give you help with key words, concepts and difficult passages.

AGENDA

6. *What is the agenda for the group meetings?*

The completed homework assignment becomes the basis for the group sharing. (However, those who don't do the homework should definitely be encouraged to come to the meeting anyway.) During the meeting the group will be guided to share on three levels: (1) TO BEGIN; (2) TO GO DEEPER; and (3) TO CLOSE.

STAYING ON TRACK

7. *How can the group get through all the material?*

Following the recommended time limits for each of the three sections will help keep you on track. Since you may not be able to answer all the questions with the time you have, you may need to skip some of them. Also, if you have more than seven people at a meeting, use the "Fearless Foursomes" described below for the Bible Study.

THE FEARLESS FOURSOME!

If you have more than seven people at a meeting, Serendipity recommends you divide into groups of 4 for the Bible Study. Count off around the group: "one, two, one, two, etc."—and have the "ones" move quickly to another room for the Bible Study. Ask one person to be the leader and follow the directions for the Bible Study time. After 30 minutes, the Group Leader will call "Time" and ask all groups to come together for the Caring Time.

GROUP BUILDING

8. *How does this course develop Group Building?*

Although this series is Serendipity's deepest Bible Study curriculum, Group Building is still essential. The group will continue "checking in" with each other and will challenge each other to grow in Christian discipleship. Working together on the group's mission should also be a very positive group-building process.

**MISSION /
MULTIPLICATION**

9. *What is the mission of a 301 group?*

Page M3 of the center section summarizes the mission of groups using this course: to commission a team from your group to start a new group. The center section will lead your group in doing this.

**LEADERSHIP
TRAINING**

10. *How do we incorporate this mission into the course?*

Page M5 of the center section gives an overview of the six steps in this process. You can either add this leadership training to the sessions a little bit at a time or in a couple of separate sessions.

**GROUP
COVENANT**

11. *What is a group covenant?*

A group covenant is a "contract" that spells out your expectations and the ground rules for your group. It's very important that your group discuss these issues—preferably as part of the first session.

**GROUND
RULES**

12. *What are the ground rules for the group?* (Check those that you agree upon.)

❏ PRIORITY: While you are in the course, you give the group meetings priority.

❏ PARTICIPATION: Everyone participates and no one dominates.

❏ RESPECT: Everyone is given the right to their own opinion and all questions are encouraged and respected.

❏ CONFIDENTIALITY: Anything that is said in the meeting is never repeated outside the meeting.

❏ EMPTY CHAIR: The group stays open to new people at every meeting as long as they understand the ground rules.

❏ SUPPORT: Permission is given to call upon each other in time of need—even in the middle of the night.

❏ ADVICE GIVING: Unsolicited advice is not allowed.

❏ MISSION: We agree to do everything in our power to start a new group as our mission (see center section).

INTRODUCTION TO THE BOOK OF 1 JOHN

John was an old man when he wrote his first epistle. All the other disciples were dead. Only he remained of the original Twelve. His long life had afforded him the opportunity to witness the spectacular growth of the church. It had begun with only a handful of disciples clustered together in Jerusalem. Now it had spread throughout the known world and the believers had become so numerous that it was difficult to number them all.

But not all that John had seen was good. As well as growth, there had been dissension, defection and heresy—even in the churches John pastored. In fact, this is why he came to write this epistle: a group of people from his church had gotten involved in strange doctrine. They had then left the church and formed their own community. Now they were trying to persuade other Christians to do the same thing—to leave and join this new group.

So John was compelled to write this letter. In fact, it was an urgent need. Soon, like the other apostles, his time would be at an end. And when he was gone, who would ensure that the church remained loyal to the teachings of Jesus? It was vital that the church understand clearly what lay at the heart of Christianity. It was vital that Christians grasp firmly the nature of the Gospel.

So John wrote his first epistle. In it one gets the sense that here John is boiling down the Gospel to its essence: "God is light; God is love; Jesus is the Messiah, the Son of God who has come in the flesh; and we are to be his children who have eternal life, who do not continue in sin, and who love one another." This is what it is all about. This is what God has been trying to teach the human race for all these hundreds of years. Here John is distilling all the wisdom and insight of his long years into a few incisive chapters. In the First Epistle of John, therefore, what we have is essential Christianity as seen by the last of the Twelve. John records his final thoughts on the nature of the faith so that, once and for all, we would get it straight. As such, John's epistle is the summation of revelation history and thus it is a book to master—with both heart and head.

Occasion

There were problems in John's church—deep ones that compelled him to write. It is difficult, of course, to reconstruct with full accuracy just what the situation was in the multiple house churches in the Ephesus area where John ministered. Still, it appears that what happened was that a group of Christians got involved in false teaching, split off from the church (2:19), and then started hassling their former friends, probably trying to convince them to espouse their new "advanced" religious views (2:26). (This is a typical response. If you can get others to agree with your newly embraced viewpoint, then you yourself feel more confident that you are, indeed, "right.") Thus John writes this epistle to refute these erroneous views and to encourage those in the church to remain faithful to the Gospel as taught by the apostles.

The error of these secessionists was twofold: they had a defective view of Jesus and a wrong view of sin. On their view of Jesus, they were so caught up with the idea of Jesus as the divine, pre-existent Lord that they almost totally neglected his human side. While they probably would not deny that Jesus was a man, to them this fact was insignificant. His humanity did not really matter in comparison to his divinity. As a result, they did not believe Jesus to be the Messiah (2:22; 5:1). In particular, they denied that Jesus, as the Son of God, had died. This was the really fatal error, because it undercut the very heart of the Gospel. The Gospel defines God as love and love as the laying down of one's life (John 15:13). If Jesus Christ, the Son of God, did not lay down his life for us, then the love of God was not revealed in Christ.

They also had an erroneous view of ethics. Specifically, they claimed to be free from sin, and free from the commandment to love others. Since they did not confess that Jesus was the Messiah, they did not feel any need to obey what he said. And since they felt that they were free from sin, they did not need the Son of God to die in their place for their sins.

These secessionists had come to think of themselves as some sort of spiritual "elite," claiming (probably by direct revelation—see 4:1–6) that they had a "deeper" understanding of Christianity than others. As an antidote to this sort of spiritual pride, John reminds his readers again and again that Christians are called upon to love one another. They are not to look down on those brothers and sisters who do not measure up to their own (supposed) superior insight.

It is not clear what, if any, "label" can be affixed to this group of secessionists. The ideas they held were probably related to what later became Gnosticism—a philosophy that taught that matter (including the body) was impure and that "spirit" was all that really counted. Therefore, it is not surprising that these secessionists, with this Gnostic view of reality, minimized the humanity of Jesus. To them salvation came via illumination. Thus esoteric "knowledge" is what they sought, instead of hearing and heeding apostolic doctrine.

Authorship

But did the apostle John actually write this epistle? This has been the assumption thus far in this introduction. Yet there are those scholars who would question whether this is so.

In fact, the author of this letter is nowhere named in 1 John. So, whatever one concludes, it is by way of speculation. However, a good case can be made that John, the beloved apostle, is indeed the author of this epistle. There are a number of reasons for attributing this anonymous epistle to him, including:

1. The strong tradition dating back to the early days of the church that John was the author.

2. The many similarities in style and content between the Gospel of John and this epistle. The same sharp contrasts appear in both—between light and darkness; truth and falsehood; love and hate. What differences do exist between the two books can be traced to differences in purpose arising out of differences in audience, since the historical context had shifted between the time of the Gospel and the time of this epistle.

3. The internal information in the epistle points to John as the author. For example, the author tells us that he was one of the original eyewitnesses of Jesus (1:1–2). Also, the author writes with the air of authority that would be expected of one who was an apostle (see 4:6).

Date

It is very difficult to fix a date to this epistle. The evidence is not clear nor conclusive. However, the best guess is that 1 John was written toward the end of the New Testament era (A.D. 90–95), by which time this Gnostic-like heresy had begun to flourish.

Style

First John is written in the simplest Greek found in all the New Testament. (It is the first book seminary students learn to translate.) There are 5,437 different Greek words that appear in the New Testament, yet in the three Johannine epistles, only 303 of these are used—5 1/2 percent of the total. This is not to say, however, that 1 John is a simple, superficial book. On the contrary, it is one of the most profound books in the entire New Testament. Perhaps because of (not despite) his simple vocabulary, John focuses in on the core of the Gospel. All else is cut away. He writes only what really matters.

A story is told by Jerome about the "blessed John the evangelist" when he was an extremely old man. According to Jerome, John now has to be carried into the worship service at Ephesus. John is unable to say anything except "little children, love one another," which he repeats over and over. The believers, having heard this same thing so often, ask: "Master, why do you always say this?" "Because," he replied, "it is enough."

Martin Luther wrote: "I have never read a book written in simpler words than this one, and yet the words are inexpressible."

Literary Form

First John is not an epistle in the sense that 2 and 3 John are (or in the sense of Paul's letters). It does not identify the writer or the recipients. In fact, there is no specific name or place mentioned anywhere in this document. There is no salutation, nor is there a final greeting. It is clear that this is intentional, since John knew perfectly well how a letter was written. Third John has been called by some the most perfect example in the New Testament of Greek letter format. Clearly, John was writing a different sort of document.

Three things are evident about John's effort

here. First, this is a literary document. John states some 13 times that he is writing (in contrast to speaking or preaching; see for example 1:4). Second, it is clear that he has a specific audience in mind, which he refers to as "you" (in the plural) some 22 times. Third, there is a so-called "double-opening" (similar to that in James), within which John states twice the themes he then develops in the rest of the manuscript. So what we have here is probably a "literary epistle"—a written document addressed to a particular audience. His audience is the community of churches in and around Ephesus that he pastored and which remained loyal to the Gospel he preached.

Structure and Theme

It is difficult to "outline" 1 John; i.e., to track the flow of the author's thought and put it into neat categories and divisions (as one can do with Romans, for example). Rather, it seems that John (much like James) would write a paragraph and then be reminded of a related topic which he would then deal with in the next paragraph. This, in turn, would spark a further thought. This is not to say that John's ideas stumble out in a haphazard fashion. This is certainly not the case. His ideas are focused and interrelated. The ideas hang together—but not by means of a western style of logic. The structure is almost spiral, "for the development of a theme often brings us back almost to the starting-point; almost but not quite, for there is a slight shift which provides a transition to a fresh theme; or it may be to a theme which had apparently been dismissed at an earlier point and now comes up for consideration from a slightly different angle" (Dodd).

John's central concern is quite clear, however. He wants to define the marks of a true Christian, over against what was being taught by the secessionists. This is very important. He wants his congregation to have the assurance that they do, indeed, have eternal life (5:13), despite what the false teachers are saying. What, then, are these "marks"? According to John Stott, the characteristics of a true Christian in 1 John are these: right belief (the doctrinal test), righteousness (the moral test), and love (the social test).

Is it possible, therefore, to capture John's exposition in outline form? Not easily! Raymond Brown identifies some 27 different attempts to outline 1 John. Still, it is highly probable that John had some structure in mind—even if we are hard put to reproduce it—since both the Gospel of John and Revelation have coherent outlines. Brown's outline is as follows and will be used in this book (with the exceptions of Units 9 and 10) to define the unit divisions:[1]

Outline

1. Prologue (1:1–4)

2. Part One (1:5–3:10)
   A. The Gospel of God as light; three boasts and three opposite hypotheses (1:5–2:2)
   B. Three claims of intimate knowledge of God to be tested by behavior (2:3–11)
   C. Admonitions to believers: having conquered the evil one, they must resist the world (2:12–17)
   D. Warning against the secessionists as antichrists who deny the Son and the Father (2:18–27)
   E. God's children versus the devil's children (2:28–3:10)

3. Part Two (3:11–5:12)
   A. The Gospel of loving one another (3:11–24)
   B. The spirits of truth and of deceit, and their respective adherents (4:1–6)
   C. Loving one another as a way of abiding in and loving God (4:7–5:4a)
   D. Faith as conqueror of the world, and the role of testimony (5:4b–12)

4. The Conclusion (5:13–21)

Further Study

1. Read through 1 John in one sitting. As you do so, list all the characteristics that you can of the false teachers. In another list, note what John defines as the essence of true religion.

2. Make a list of all the warnings that John gives in this epistle.

3. Underline each time John uses the word "love." What does he teach about love in this epistle?

Second and Third John

These two short epistles are covered in Units 12 and 13. The date these letters were written is uncertain, but was probably in the late A.D. 80s or early 90s. This is when the heresy which is rebuked here (an early form of Gnosticism) began to flourish and false prophets were roaming the countryside looking for hospitality. John addresses the problem of these wandering missionaries in 2 and 3 John (see Summaries on pages 58 and 62).

COMMENTS
Irenaeus' Second-Century Account of the Apostle John

But Polycarp also was not only instructed by apostles, and conversed with many who had seen Christ, but was also, by apostles in Asia, appointed bishop of the Church in Smyrna, whom I also saw in my early youth, for he tarried [on earth] a very long time, and, when a very old man, gloriously and most nobly suffering martyrdom, departed this life, having always taught the things which he had learned from the apostles, and which the Church has handed down, and which alone are true. To these things all the Asiatic Churches testify, as do also those men who have succeeded Polycarp down to the present time,—a man who was of much greater weight, and a more steadfast witness of truth, than Valentinus, and Marcion, and the rest of the heretics. He it was who, coming to Rome in the time of Anicetus caused many to turn away from the aforesaid heretics to the Church of God, proclaiming that he had received this one and sole truth from the apostles,—that, namely, which is handed down by the Church. There are also those who heard from him that John, the disciple of the Lord, going to bathe at Ephesus, and perceiving Cerinthus within, rushed out of the bath-house without bathing, exclaiming, "Let us fly, lest even the bath-house fall down, because Cerinthus, the enemy of the truth, is within." And Polycarp himself replied to Marcion, who met him on one occasion, and said, "Dost thou know me?" "I do know thee, the first-born of Satan." Such was the horror which the apostles and their disciples had against holding even verbal communication with any corrupters of the truth; as Paul also says, "A man that is a heretic, after the first and second admonition, reject; knowing that he that is such is subverted, and sinneth, being condemned of himself." There is also a very powerful Epistle of Polycarp written to the Philippians, from which those who choose to do so, and are anxious about their salvation, can learn the character of his faith, and the preaching of the truth. Then, again, the Church in Ephesus, founded by Paul, and having John remaining among them permanently until the times of Trajan, is a true witness of the tradition of the apostles.—Taken from *Ante-Nicene Fathers: History of the Christian Church*, Vol. 1, page 416, by Irenaeus.

¹Raymond E. Brown, "The Epistles of John," *The Anchor Bible* (Garden City, NY: Doubleday & Company, 1982), pp. xx-xxi.

UNIT 1—The Word of Life / 1 John 1:1–4

1 *That which was from the beginning, which we have heard, which we have seen with our eyes, which we have looked at and our hands have touched—this we proclaim concerning the Word of life.* ²*The life appeared; we have seen it and testify to it, and we proclaim to you the eternal life, which was with the Father and has appeared to us.* ³*We proclaim to you what we have seen and heard, so that you also may have fellowship with us. And our fellowship is with the Father and with his Son, Jesus Christ.* ⁴*We write this to make our*ᵃ *joy complete.*

ᵃ4 Some manuscripts *your*

READ

Two readings of the passage are suggested—each with a response to be checked or filled in on the worksheet.

First Reading / First Impressions: To get familiar with the passage, read the passage through without stopping and record your "first impressions."

Read through the entire letter and check two boxes that best describe the tone or word of this letter.

- ❏ scholarly—like a professor
- ❏ pious—like a devotional writer
- ❏ fatherly—like a parent
- ❏ formal—like an IRS form letter
- ❏ stern—like a Marine drill sergeant
- ❏ diplomatic—like a politician
- ❏ tender—like a love letter
- ❏ friendly—like an alumni newsletter
- ❏ sober—like a bank officer
- ❏ long-winded—like a preacher

Second Reading / Theme or Big Idea: To get the overall idea, thought or "gist" of the passage, read the passage slowly as though you are seeing the action from the press box—high above the stadium.

Read the first four verses (1 John 1:1–4) and check the boxes that best describe the "big idea" in this passage. (Choose two.)

- ❏ Are you ready for this?
- ❏ God has a better idea.
- ❏ Check it out.
- ❏ Oh what a feeling.
- ❏ Fellowship is what it is all about.
- ❏ Reach out and touch.
- ❏ Who said you can't have it all?
- ❏ Just one look. That's all it took.
- ❏ Let the good times roll.
- ❏ I'm gonna make you an offer you can't refuse.

SEARCH

The apostle John could claim to have heard, seen and even touched the "Word of life." Look up the following verses and jot down what each contributed to his first-hand experience.

1. John leaves John the Baptist to follow Jesus (John 1:35–39—John usually didn't mention his own name or referred to himself as "the disciple whom Jesus loved").

2. John is present at the Transfiguration (Mark 9:2–13).

3. John is with Jesus at Gethsemane (Mark 14:32–42).

4. John is present at the crucifixion of Jesus (John 19:26–27).

5. John discovers the empty tomb (John 20:1–9).

6. What is the significance of the ways John personally experienced "the Word" (vv. 1–2; see notes)?

7. Given why John wrote this letter (vv. 3–4; see notes), what do you expect to gain from studying it?

APPLY

1. As you begin this course, what are some goals you would like to work on? Check one or two from the list below and add another if you wish.
   ❐ to get to know God in a more personal way
   ❐ to understand what I believe as a Christian and where I stand on issues
   ❐ to develop my skills in Bible study and personal devotions
   ❐ to belong to a small group that will support me in my growth
   ❐ to think through my values and priorities in light of God's will
   ❐ to wrestle with the next step in my spiritual journey with others who care

2. What are you willing to commit to in the way of disciplines during the time you are in this course?
   ❐ to complete the Bible study home assignment before the group meets
   ❐ to attend the group meetings except in cases of emergency
   ❐ to share in leading the group—taking my turn in rotation
   ❐ to keep confidential anything that is shared in the group
   ❐ to reach out to others who are not in a group and invite them to join us
   ❐ to participate in the group's mission of "giving birth" to a new group (see center section)

GROUP AGENDA

Every group meeting has three parts: (1) To Begin (10–15 minutes) to break the ice; (2) To Go Deeper (30 minutes) for Bible Study; and (3) To Close (15–30 minutes) for caring and prayer. When you get to the second part, have someone read the Scripture out loud and then divide into groups of 4 (4 at the dining table, 4 at the kitchen table, etc.). Then have everyone come back together for the third part.

TO BEGIN / 10–15 Min. (Choose 1 or 2)

1. What was special to you about your room in the first house you can remember living in?

2. What childhood memory is as clear today as the day it happened?

3. What person you met as a child made a lasting impression on your life?

TO GO DEEPER / 30 Min. (Choose 2 or 3)

1. Why did John write this epistle, and why is it important for us to study it? (Read the first four paragraphs of the Introduction on page 8.)

2. Why does John make a point of his first-hand experience with Jesus? Why is it important that Jesus was "heard," "seen" and "touched"?

3. When did Jesus become more than just a name to you?

4. When have you been part of a group where you enjoyed true Christian fellowship—with mutual love and understanding?

5. CASE STUDY: Mary calls you to say she is attending a meditation workshop sponsored by a New Age group because she realizes her need for a spiritual center for her life. From your experience, what could you honestly share with her regarding spiritual reality?

TO CLOSE / 15–30 Min.

1. What did you check in the first question in APPLY for the goals you would like to work on during this course? (If you have answered #7 in SEARCH, you may want to share that response.)

2. What disciplines are you willing to commit to (second question in APPLY)?

3. What is holding back your joy from being "complete" (v. 4)?

4. How would you like this group to pray for you?

14

NOTES

Summary. John begins his letter with a prologue that is reminiscent of the prologue to his Gospel (John 1:1–18). Both prologues focus on the pre-existent Word of God who has been revealed to humanity. In each there are the themes of "life" and "witness." In each, there is the visual manifestation of God to the "we" who then proclaim what has been experienced. But there are also differences between the two prologues. In the Gospel prologue, the emphasis is on the divine nature of the Word. Over half the verses make this point. But in the prologue to 1 John, the divine nature of the Word is simply noted. Instead, the emphasis is on the *physical manifestation* of the Word of God. This difference in emphasis is due to the difference in audiences. In his Gospel, John wrote to Jews who did not believe that God could or would reveal himself in the person of Jesus. But here in the epistle, the secessionists (who were false teachers) presuppose that Jesus is the Son of God. Their problem is that they neglect his human side. This is why John emphasizes the fact that the pre-existent Word of life has been experienced by auditory, visual and manual means. The Word really became flesh—real flesh.

John's method of writing is not haphazard. It has a distinct purpose. John focuses attention on the object which is proclaimed (Jesus Christ), rather than on the act of proclamation itself.

1:1 Although this document lacks the usual identification of sender and recipient, as well as the normal greeting and prayer, it is clear that this is not an anonymous tract written to a general audience. Scattered throughout the letter are abundant personal comments and specific references (e.g., 2:19). This letter was written to particular people living at a particular place who were dealing with specific problems. (For an example of how NT letters generally begin, see 1 Peter 1:1–2 and Philippians 1:1–2.)

which. John begins with four clauses, each introduced by "which." The first clause describes who the "Word of life" is. The next three describe how he was experienced.

from the beginning. The initial clause makes the astonishing assertion that this "Word of life" was pre-existent (see John 1:1). Since only divine beings pre-existed, in this way John affirms the deity of Jesus.

heard / seen / touched. However, John's emphasis in this letter is on the human nature of Jesus. The next three clauses describe how his physical presence was experienced. This eternal "Word of life" took on a form so specific and so concrete that he could be known by means of the physical senses. Notice the progression of experience. In the Old Testament, men and women had on many occasions *heard* God; occasionally they had *seen* some aspect of God (see Ex. 3:1–6; 33:18–23); but no one had ever *touched* God. This was the final proof that the Word of life had indeed been "made flesh and dwelt among us" (John 1:14, KJV). In Greek courts, the testimony of two senses was required in order to verify that something occurred (Brown). John offers evidence from a third sense as well. He emphasizes as strongly as he can the physical existence of Jesus because of the secessionists lack of interest in the earthly Jesus.

touched. This word means literally "to feel after" or "to grope," as a blind person might do. It also means "to examine closely" (Brooke). Jesus was no phantom. He was a real person whose skin could be touched.

Word of life. This phrase refers both to the message preached by the early Christians and to the content of that message. The message preached by the apostles and by Jesus himself concerned eternal life (i.e., spiritual life—that which people do not naturally possess but which must be given them by God). This is one sense of the phrase "Word of life." But Jesus not only preached this message. He *was* the message. This is the second sense of the phrase. The "Word of life" was preached to people, which was that Jesus Christ was the Word of God, the very embodiment of eternal life itself (see John 1:4; 11:25–26; 14:6).

1:2 This is a parenthesis in which John declares in unequivocal terms that *Jesus* is the Word he is talking about.

we. The author is among those who knew Jesus personally.

testify. This is a legal term describing what an eyewitness does while in court. Such a person makes a public declaration of what he or she has experienced first-hand.

the eternal life. This is a curious way by which to refer to Jesus. Yet in this way John focuses on what is so significant about Jesus: he is life itself. God's very life has appeared in the historical person of Jesus (see John 1:2).

1:3 *We proclaim.* This is the main verb of the opening sentence. It clarifies the intention of the prologue. John's aim is to identify the nature of the apostolic proclamation, which is that Jesus is the incarnate God.

fellowship. This word means literally, in Greek, "having in common." It has the dual sense of first, *participation together* in shared activity or outlook, and second, *union together* because of this shared experience. The aim of John's testimony is to bring others into participation and union with him and his colleagues, and thus into participation and union with the Father and the Son. The secessionists proposed a different sort of union (or communion). Their emphasis was on direct union with God, whereas John emphasizes communion not only with God but with others. John identifies a triangular pattern of relationship (God, self, others) in contrast to their vertical pattern (God and self).

with the Father and with his Son. Apparently the false teachers were saying that it was possible to have fellowship with God apart from Christ. John's point is that fellowship with God is possible only through Jesus (2:23), because in him eternal life (i.e., God's life) is manifested.

1:4 John identifies his second reason for writing. He wants his own joy to be completed.

joy. This is the profound gladness or satisfaction that comes when one participates in the life of God. This is an important term for John. He uses it nine times in his Gospel (along with an additional nine times that he uses the verb "rejoice"). See, for example, John 15:11; 16:20,22,24; and 17:13—each of which promises joy. In John 20:20 he indicates that the fulfillment of this promise is found in the experience of the resurrected Lord. Here, in 1 John, he goes one step further and indicates that the joy which began with the experience of the resurrected Lord is brought to completion via the experience of this full-orbed fellowship between Father, Son and the children of God. The children of God include the apostles and those who have believed the Good News which they proclaimed about Jesus.

complete. Full, lacking nothing.

UNIT 2—Walking in the Light / 1 John 1:5–2:2

Walking in the Light

⁵**This is the message we have heard from him and declare to you: God is light; in him there is no darkness at all. ⁶If we claim to have fellowship with him yet walk in the darkness, we lie and do not live by the truth. ⁷But if we walk in the light, as he is in the light, we have fellowship with one another, and the blood of Jesus, his Son, purifies us from all**ᵃ **sin.**

⁸**If we claim to be without sin, we deceive ourselves and the truth is not in us. ⁹If we confess our sins, he is faithful and just and will forgive us our sins and purify us from all unrighteous-** ness. ¹⁰**If we claim we have not sinned, we make him out to be a liar and his word has no place in our lives.**

2 **My dear children, I write this to you so that you will not sin. But if anybody does sin, we have one who speaks to the Father in our defense—Jesus Christ, the Righteous One. ²He is the atoning sacrifice for our sins, and not only for ours but also for**ᵇ **the sins of the whole world.**

ᵃ7 Or *every*   ᵇ2 Or *He is the one who turns aside God's wrath, taking away our sins, and not only ours but also*

READ

First Reading / First Impressions: This passage strikes me as:

❏ a manifesto of the Christian life   ❏ a back and forth argument
❏ a pastor's letter to encourage the church   ❏ a simple passage that is really very complete

Second Reading / Big Idea: What verse seems to be the controlling verse of this section? Why?

SEARCH

1. What does John mean by his statement "God is light" (v. 5; see note)?

2. Verses 6–10 are a series of "if" statements. What is the condition and result in each instance?

	Condition	Result
(v. 6)		
(v. 7)		
(v. 8)		
(v. 9)		
(v. 10)		

3. What does it mean practically to "walk in the light" (v. 7), and how can you tell if you are doing so (see notes)?

4. What modern example might you use to explain 2:1–2 to someone unfamiliar with the Old Testament ritual of atonement (see Lev. 16:6–22,34)?

APPLY

From now on in the APPLY part of the worksheet, you will be asked to try various forms of application. In this unit, try rewriting a verse of Scripture in your own words. This will force you to think through the meaning as you write your own paraphrase. Go back and read verse 9—phrase by phrase. Close your eyes and try to restate the thought of this verse in your own everyday speech, like you were explaining this idea to your next-door neighbor. Then, in the space below write your own original (and perhaps expanded) paraphrase. Use a little "literary license" if you wish, but get the main idea of verse 9 across.

What help do the following verses give you as you deal with sin in your life?

1:9

2:1–2

GROUP AGENDA

Every group meeting has three parts: (1) To Begin (10–15 minutes) to break the ice; (2) To Go Deeper (30 minutes) for Bible Study; and (3) To Close (15–30 minutes) for caring and prayer. When you get to the second part, have someone read the Scripture out loud and then divide into groups of 4 (4 at the dining table, 4 at the kitchen table, etc.). Then have everyone come back together for the third part.

TO BEGIN / 10–15 Min. (Choose 1 or 2)

1. Have you ever been afraid of the dark?

2. When was the last time the lights went out in your house and you were plunged into darkness?

3. Who came to your defense when you got in trouble as a kid?

TO GO DEEPER / 30 Min. (Choose 2 or 3)

1. According to 2:1, what is John's hope for believers? In actuality, what is the reality?

2. What hope does John give when people fail to live according to God's light?

3. What is God's part and what is your part in the confession process?

4. This letter provides three tests for the Christian life: (a) the moral test, (b) the social test, and (c) the doctrinal test. Which test is discussed here and what is the conclusion?

5. CASE STUDY: Judy has a problem with guilt. Spiritually she cleaned house last year, but she keeps hearing voices from her past life, reminding her of her sin. How would you help Judy deal with her guilt?

TO CLOSE / 15–30 Min.

1. Who could you invite to this group next week?

2. Share what you wrote for one or both of the exercises in APPLY.

3. Have you been walking lately more in the light or in the darkness?

4. How can the group pray for you?

NOTES

Summary. In the prologue, John declares his hope that all may be in fellowship with God and with each other. Here in these verses, he examines the barrier that prevents such fellowship (i.e., sin) and how to deal with it. By means of a series of "if/then" clauses (with the "then" implied) he identifies three erroneous views of sin which he then evaluates on the basis of the fact that God is light. His pattern of writing is to begin a sentence with "if" and then state the false view and its detrimental consequences (vv. 6,8,10). He then starts a new sentence, again with the word "if," within which he states the correct view (vv. 7,9; 2:1b).

1:5 *from him.* John is quite clear about the source of his message. What he preaches comes directly from Jesus, taught to him as one of the Twelve. In contrast, the secessionist's wisdom is derived from inner, subjective visions (as implied in 4:1–3).

God is light. This is John's second great assertion about God. His first assertion was that *God had come in the flesh* (vv. 1–3). Here he states that *God is light.* Within contemporary Greek culture, "light" was a common symbol for God. It conveyed the idea of wisdom, integrity, excellence, etc. Within the context of the Bible, "light" was connected to two basic ideas. First, on the intellectual level, it was a symbol of truth. John is saying that God is truth. God illuminates the understanding of people. He reveals the right answer and the correct way (see Psalm 27:1 and Prov. 6:23). Second, on the moral level, light is a symbol of purity. John is saying that God is righteous and holy (see Isa. 5:20; Rom. 13:11–14; Eph. 5:8–14). He is good, not evil. The coming of Jesus was, therefore, the coming of light (see Matt. 4:16; John 1:4–9; 3:19–21). Jesus is "the light," as John says in his Gospel. He is the incarnation of the divine light (John 8:12; 9:5). This insight into the nature of God stands in sharp contrast to the many "dark gods" known in the first-century world who were given over more to evil than to good.

1:6 *If we claim.* This is the first of three false claims that John will refute. He will measure the validity of each of these claims against the apostolic proclamation that God is light and in him is no darkness.

to have fellowship ... yet walk in the darkness. It is claimed by the false teachers that it is possible to be in union with God and yet habitually sin. That this cannot be so is clear from what John has just stated about God. If God is *light* then, by definition, those who walk in *darkness* cannot be part of him.

This was a common Gnostic error. They felt that since the body was insignificant, then it did not matter what a person did. The true essence of the person—the "spirit"—remained untouched and thus uncontaminated by sin.

we lie. John moves from the false proposition (that they have fellowship with God even while living in darkness) to the inevitable conclusion (they are not telling the truth). To say that one can practice sin and still be in fellowship with God is simply not true.

1:7 But if. Having identified the false proposition of the secessionists in verse 6, John now states the true proposition in verse 7.

walk in the light. The image here is of a person confidently striding forth, illuminated by the light of God's truth, in contrast to the person who stumbles around in darkness. To "walk in the light" is to be open and transparent. It is "to be, so to speak, all of a piece, to have nothing to conceal, and to make no attempt to conceal anything" (Stephen Neill).

purifies. If the first result of "walking in the light" is fellowship with one another, the second result is cleansing from sin. That which causes the blemish of sin to disappear is the sacrificial death of Jesus. (This is what the symbol of "blood" refers to.) It is through the death of Jesus that sin is forgiven and forgotten. The verb tense indicates that this purification occurs not just once, but is a continuous process.

1:8 If we claim to be without sin. The second false claim: that they are sinless. It is one thing to deny that sin breaks fellowship with God (as in vv. 6—7). At least then the existence of sin is admitted even if its impact is denied. But it is another thing to deny the fact of sin altogether. This might have been the response of the secessionists to John's assertion (in v. 6) that because they walked in the darkness of sin they could have no fellowship with God. "But," they would protest, "this cannot be so. We do not walk in the darkness of sin. In fact, we have no sin at all."

we deceive ourselves. This assertion goes beyond a mere lie (v. 6). This is self-deception. They really believed they were without sin.

the truth is not in us. Not only do they not live by the truth (v. 6), but by such a claim they demonstrate that they do not even know the truth (as found, for example, in Rom. 3:23—"all have sinned"). Again, this demonstrates that they are not part of God, who is light, and who therefore stands for truth.

1:9 If we confess our sins. As in verse 7, after naming the problem, John then states the antidote. Rather than denying their sinful natures, they need to admit their sin to God and so gain forgiveness.

faithful. God will keep his promise to forgive (Mic. 7:18–20).

just. The granting of forgiveness is not merely an act of unanticipated mercy but a response of justice, since the conditions for forgiveness have been fulfilled as a result of the death of Christ.

purify. Sin makes a person unclean; forgiveness washes away that sin (see v. 7).

1:10 If we claim we have not sinned. The third false claim: not only do they say that at the present moment they are without sin (v. 8), they actually claim never to have sinned! The secessionists might admit that sin does break fellowship with God (v. 6) and that all people have an inborn sinful nature (v. 8), but they would still deny that they, in fact, have ever actually sinned.

we make him out to be a liar. God's verdict is that all people are sinners. Furthermore, he says that it is through the death of Christ that he forgives sin. So by claiming sinlessness they are, in essence, saying that God is lying about human nature and about his claim to forgive people.

his word has no place in our lives. They claim to know God and yet they do not walk in his way nor accept his viewpoint about human nature. Therefore, contrary to what they might claim, they are, in fact, alienated from God (see John 8:44).

2:1 dear children. This is literally "small children," an affectionate term for his congregation which John uses frequently (2:12,28; 3:7,18; 4:4; 5:21). At this point in his letter John shifts his focus from the secessionists and their heresy to his own flock and their needs.

if anybody does sin. While urging sinlessness as a goal to strive for, John knows that in this present life this cannot be achieved. So the issue then is how to deal with sin. The answer is found in the triple role of Jesus as the advocate, the Righteous One, and the atoning sacrifice.

Righteous One. John frequently refers to Jesus by means of this term (e.g., 2:29; 3:7). Jesus is righteous both in the sense of being an example to follow and, especially, in the sense of not being contaminated by personal sin.

UNIT 3—Walking in Love / 1 John 2:3-11

³*We know that we have come to know him if we obey his commands. ⁴The man who says, "I know him," but does not do what he commands is a liar, and the truth is not in him. ⁵But if anyone obeys his word, God's love^a is truly made complete in him. This is how we know we are in him: ⁶Whoever claims to live in him must walk as Jesus did.*

⁷*Dear friends, I am not writing you a new command but an old one, which you have had since the beginning. This old command is the message you have heard. ⁸Yet I am writing you a new command; its truth is seen in him and you,* because the darkness is passing and the true light is already shining.

⁹*Anyone who claims to be in the light but hates his brother is still in the darkness. ¹⁰Whoever loves his brother lives in the light, and there is nothing in him^b to make him stumble. ¹¹But whoever hates his brother is in the darkness and walks around in the darkness; he does not know where he is going, because the darkness has blinded him.*

^a5 Or *word, love for God*   ^b10 Or *it*

READ

First Reading / First Impressions: My sense here is that John:

❒ is stating the obvious

❒ has succeeded in distilling the essence of Christianity

❒ is deeply profound

❒ is confusing me

Second Reading / Big Idea: What's the main point or topic?

SEARCH

1. What connections can you find between obeying, knowing and loving God in verses 3–6 (see also John 14:15,21,23–24)?

2. Since the false teachers were bringing "new insights" to these people, what does John mean by stressing that his command is not "new" (v. 7; see note)?

3. From Mark 12:28–31 (also Lev. 19:18; Deut. 6:5) and John 15:12,17, what is this "old command" to which John refers (see also 3:11; 2 John 5)?

4. From what you can recall from the Gospels, what are a couple ways Jesus made this "old" command new (v. 8; see notes)?

5. What does John's linking of "love/light" and "hate/darkness" together (vv. 9–11) imply about a person's relationship with God and their spiritual condition?

APPLY

Measuring yourself in the past few weeks by verses 3 and 6, what grade would you give yourself for the test—Do you obey God?_____ What grade would you give yourself in the past few weeks for the test in verse 10—Do you love others?_____ What is one specific way these verses challenge you to grow in your life?

Take inventory of the following areas in your life and put an **"X"** on the lines below to indicate how you are feeling right now about each of these areas—somewhere between the two extremes. For instance, you might put the **"X"** on EMOTIONAL LIFE right in the middle because you are halfway between "Blues in the Night" and "Feeling Groovy."

IN MY EMOTIONAL LIFE, I'M FEELING LIKE ...
Blues in the Night _____**Feeling Groovy**

IN MY CLOSE RELATIONSHIPS, I'M FEELING LIKE ...
Stormy Weather _____**The Sound of Music**

IN MY WORK, SCHOOL OR CAREER, I'M FEELING LIKE ...
Take This Job and Shove It _____**The Future's So Bright, I Gotta Wear "Shades"**

IN MY SPIRITUAL LIFE, I'M FEELING LIKE ...
Sounds of Silence _____**Hallelujah Chorus**

GROUP AGENDA

Every group meeting has three parts: (1) To Begin (10–15 minutes) to break the ice; (2) To Go Deeper (30 minutes) for Bible Study; and (3) To Close (15–30 minutes) for caring and prayer. When you get to the second part, have someone read the Scripture out loud and then divide into groups of 4 (4 at the dining table, 4 at the kitchen table, etc.). Then have everyone come back together for the third part.

TO BEGIN / 10–15 Min. (Choose 1 or 2)

1. On a scale of 1 (totally rebellious) to 10 (totally compliant), how "obedient" were you as a child?

2. How much did you fight with your sibling(s)? What did you usually fight about?

3. What game did you play as a child where you were blindfolded? What was the experience like?

TO GO DEEPER / 30 Min. (Choose 2 or 3)

1. What do you think is going on in the church to cause John to write this?

2. Based on the homework and study notes, how would you say the command to love God and others can be new and old at the same time?

3. Verse 6 says, "Whoever claims to live in him must walk as Jesus did." To guide your own life, how often do you ask yourself, "What would Jesus do?"

4. Thinking about the example and teachings of Jesus, what comes to mind as particularly difficult for you to follow?

5. CASE STUDY: Bob has a problem with a grudge against his old business partner. Bob had the money. His partner had the idea. The business went sour and Bob lost his investment. Bob grumbles aloud that his partner mismanaged the business and tampered with the books to hide his mistakes. What do you say to Bob?

TO CLOSE / 15–30 Min.

1. Has your group started on the six steps toward fulfilling your mission—from the center section?

2. What "grades" did you give yourself in the first question in APPLY?

3. Share your self-inventory from the second part of APPLY.

4. How can the group pray for you?

NOTES

Summary. John now shifts his focus. He had been addressing the secessionists by way of refuting their false claims. Now he addresses his own flock, exhorting them to follow God's commands. He does, however, point out several additional false claims (see vv. 4,6,9) within the context of his discussion of the commandment to love. Within this unit John identifies two "tests" by which people can be certain they actually know God: the test of obedience and the test of love. Those who truly know God live in his way and love as Jesus loved.

2:3–6 Thus far John has presented two truths about God which lie at the heart of the apostolic proclamation and by which the accuracy of ideas and actions are to be judged. These are, first, the "... historical manifestation of the Eternal and secondly ... the fact that God is light. ... All Christian profession may be judged in relation to these truths. No thought or action can be condoned which is inconsistent either with God's nature as pure, self-giving, or with His historical palpable self-disclosure in Christ. ... This general introduction ... is now particularized in three tests—moral (the test of obedience), social (the test of love) and doctrinal (the test of belief in Christ)" (Stott). The first application of the moral test is here in verses 3–6.

2:3 We know. The New English Bible translates this opening phrase: "Here is the test by which we can make sure we know him ... ."

have come to know him. Previously John has spoken about *having fellowship with God* (see 1:3,6,7). Now he speaks about the parallel concept, that of *knowing God* (see 2:4,13–14; 3:6,16; 4:16). The verb tense indicates that he is thinking about a past experience ("we have come to know him").

if we obey his commands. The first test as to whether a person knows God, therefore, is moral in nature: does that person keep God's commands? To know God is to live in his way. The secessionists claim to know God but, as John will show, they live in a way that belies that claim.

commands. The nature of these commands is not spelled out, but the context (vv. 7–11) indicates that John probably had in mind the "great commandment" to love God and love others (Mark 12:29–31). Whatever their specific definition may be, these commands are not some external semi-arbitrary set of rules which must be obeyed simply because they exist. These commands describe the way Jesus lived (see 2:6). They are the very pattern of the Life that John is talking about. They are what love looks like in a person's life. Unless the commands are seen in this way they will degenerate into dead ethical propositions.

2:4 *The man who says.* John identifies another false claim. Those who assert that they really "know God" and yet do not keep his commandments are, in fact, lying. Such a man demonstrates by what he does that what he says is false.

does not do. The emphasis here is on sins of omission (not doing) in contrast to 1:6, where the emphasis is on sins of commission (walking in darkness).

2:5 *God's love.* This is the reward for obedience. God's love reaches its fulfillment in that person's life.

made complete. The verb which John uses here means ongoing fulfillment rather than static termination.

2:6 Here John introduces the idea of the "imitation of Christ." Christians are habitually to live the way Jesus lived. He is their model. As he walked, so should they walk.

live in him. This is the third phrase which John uses to describe union with God. (In 1:3 he spoke about having "fellowship" with God, and in 2:3 he spoke about "knowing" God.) To "exist in" God or to "abide in" him "suggests an intensely personal knowledge of God; it presupposes an intimate and committed relationship with him, through Jesus, which is both permanent and continuous" (Smalley).

2:7–11 If the first test of whether one is actually a Christian is moral in nature (Do you obey God?), then the second test (given here) is relational in orientation (Do you love others?).

2:7 *Dear friends.* This is literally "beloved," and is derived from the word "love" (*agape*) which is John's focus in this section.

I am not writing you a new command. This is not a new commandment because Jesus himself had stated it some years earlier and the Johannine Christians themselves had been taught it right from the beginning of their Christian walk. It is also not new in that when Jesus gave this command he was, in fact, quoting the Old Testament. He combined Leviticus 19:18 and Deuteronomy 6:5 to form the "great commandment."

2:8 *Yet I am writing you a new command.* The commandment is new in the sense that Jesus tied together two previously separate commands (that of loving God and loving others) and broadened their application. (Christians are to love everyone, not just those in their own group as shown in the parable of the Good Samaritan in Luke 10:30–37.)

its truth is seen in him and you. It is also new in that it was only in recent years that the commandment was actually lived out by Jesus and his followers. In them one saw (instead of just read about) this new kind of love (see John 10:14–18; 15:9–17).

true light. This is genuine light, in contrast to the false "light" claimed by the secessionists. This is "true light" because what it appears to be is what it actually is. Nothing is hidden. Nothing is dark.

2:9–10 John here links sets of contrasting images: light and darkness with love and hate. Those who are in the light, love. Those who are in the darkness, hate. In other words, enlightenment goes hand in hand with active care for others.

2:9 *brother.* John's primary focus here is on love and hate within the Christian community. However, the relationships between people in the church ought to be a model for all relationships.

2:10 *loves.* The Greek word John uses here is *agape*. In Greek, there are several words that can be translated by the English word "love." There is one word for sexual attraction or sexual desire (*eros*); another for family love, affection and friendship (*philia*). In contrast, *agape* refers to self-giving sacrificial action done on behalf of another who is in need, regardless of what it might cost ("Greater love has no one than this, that he lay down his life for his friends"—John 15:13), or what is felt about that other person ("Love your enemies"—Luke 6:27).

2:11 *hates.* If a person does not love, that is, does not care for the needs of another in direct, active ways, then such a person hates. It is either love or hate in John's view. He does not offer neutrality as a comfortable third option in relationships. In the same way John describes love in terms of deeds, not feelings, so too "hate" has little to do with feelings of hostility toward others. "Hate" is the lack of loving deeds done on their behalf.

blinded. Living apart from God's way (i.e., "in darkness") will yield over time moral and spiritual blindness so that it becomes difficult for one to see what is and is not true or good. Hatred distorts perception.

UNIT 4—Stages of Faith / 1 John 2:12-17

12I write to you, dear children,
because your sins have been forgiven on
account of his name.
13I write to you, fathers,
because you have known him who is from
the beginning.
I write to you, young men,
because you have overcome the evil one.
I write to you, dear children,
because you have known the Father.
14I write to you fathers,
because you have known him who is from
the beginning.
I write to you, young men,
because you are strong,
and the word of God lives in you,
and you have overcome the evil one.

Do Not Love the World

15Do not love the world or anything in the
world. If anyone loves the world, the love of the
Father is not in him. 16For everything in the
world—the cravings of sinful man, the lust of his
eyes and the boasting of what he has and
does—comes not from the Father but from the
world. 17The world and its desires pass away, but
the man who does the will of God lives forever.

READ

First Reading / First Impressions: What's going on here?

❑ Maybe John's quoting a song.

❑ Maybe some copyist wrote some of this material down twice.

❑ Maybe John is repeating himself for emphasis.

Second Reading / Big Idea: What verse seems most important here to you? Why?

SEARCH

1. How would you describe the "children" stage of faith (vv. 12–13; see notes)?

2. How would you describe the "young men" stage of faith (vv. 13–14; see notes)?

3. How would you describe the "fathers" stage of faith (vv. 13–14; see notes)?

4. What do you think it means to "love the world" (v. 15; see notes)?

5. How have the forms of "love for the world" (v. 16) manifested themselves in your experience?

6. What are the two options a Christian has and what is the end result of each option (v. 17)?

Option 1

Option 2

APPLY
In your spiritual life, in what ways do you feel like a:

"child"—just beginning to catch on?

"young man"—at the peak of strength?

"father"—a seasoned veteran?

In what areas of your life does love for the world compete with love for God?

☐ physical desires   ☐ relationships
☐ material desires   ☐ ambitions
☐ priorities / use of time   ☐ other:_____

What is one way you can nurture the love of God in your life instead?

GROUP AGENDA

After the first part, read the Scripture out loud and divide into groups of 4. Then come back together for the third part.

TO BEGIN / 10–15 Min. (Choose 1 or 2)

1. What nickname did your parents have for you as a child that you would do a slow burn over if anyone called you now?

2. Who is the person who saves all the pictures of your family to show off at family reunions?

3. What do you crave that is either "illegal, immoral or fattening"?

TO GO DEEPER / 30 Min. (Choose 2 or 3)

1. Based on the homework questions and reference notes, what would you say marks each stage of maturity described in verses 12–14?

2. What does John mean by "the world"? Are all human desires contrary to God's will? Why?

3. As time goes on, do you find yourself more attracted or less attracted by what the "world" has to offer?

4. What encouragement for Christian living do you get from this passage?

5. CASE STUDY: Jeff, a recent college graduate, is trying to figure out his priorities regarding finances. There are so many things he needs and wants, but he is also aware of his responsibility to support the church and care for the poor. From your experience, how would you help him sort through the "love of the world" versus the love of God?

TO CLOSE / 15–30 Min.

1. Has your group taken the survey for small groups in your church (see page M15 in the center section)? If so, what are you going to do as a result?

2. How did you answer the first part of APPLY?

3. If you feel comfortable doing so, share your responses to the last two parts of APPLY. (You may also want to share your answers to #5 in SEARCH.)

4. How can the group support you in prayer?

NOTES

Summary. In contrast to those who walk in darkness—and about whom John has just been writing (2:9–11)—he now turns to those who are committed to the light. He has two things to say to the Christian community. First, he assures them of their standing before God (vv. 12–14); and second, he warns them about loving the world (vv. 15–17). It is worth noting that up to this point in his epistle John has always led off his argument by first stating false claims, but here his focus is on true claims.

2:12–14 In six parallel and almost poetic statements John addresses three groups of Christians by using the terminology of a family. It is not completely clear to whom John is referring with the titles "children," "fathers," and "young men." In fact, he may not have actual groups in mind and is simply thinking about different stages of the spiritual life (the innocence of childhood, the strength of youth, and the mature knowledge of age, as Augustine put it). Some scholars feel that John is addressing the whole community by means of the term "dear children," much as the wisdom teachers of the Old Testament addressed their followers. He then speaks to two groups of believers within the community of "dear children": those who have been Christians for a long time (the fathers) and those who are newer members of the faith (the young men).

2:12 *children.* John affirms two foundational truths: they are forgiven (v. 12) and they do know God (v. 13c). It is important that the Christians in John's church be assured this is true for them. The secessionists are claiming that they have experienced forgiveness and that they know God, but John has rejected their claims (1:6–10; 2:4). Lest his own flock fear their claims to such reality are also being rejected, John assures them that they are in a different place from the secessionists. Here he reaffirms that the walk of faith begins with these two experiences.

have been forgiven. The verb tense indicates that John is thinking of the forgiveness that comes at the time of conversion, whereas in 1:9 his concern was with ongoing forgiveness for subsequent sins based on the confession of sins.

name. In the Near East a name is very significant. It is not just a convenient word for distinguishing one person from another. It is a description of the essential character of that person. Thus, the name Jesus recalls not just who he is but his atoning work through which forgiveness has been made possible (1:7; 2:1–2).

2:13 fathers. "[These are the] spiritually adult in the congregation. Their first flash of ecstasy in receiving forgiveness and fellowship with the Father was an experience of long ago. Even the battles of the young man, to which he will next refer, are past. The fathers have progressed into a deep communion with God" (Stott).

you have known him. The message to the "fathers" here and in verse 14 is identical. John reassures them that they do, indeed, know Christ. Once again, John uses the perfect tense for the verb. In this way he emphasizes the present consequences of a past event. This same tense is used for each of the main verbs in the six messages.

him who is from the beginning. The reference is probably to Jesus since it echoes the phrase by which John opens his letter: "that which was from the beginning" which is a direct reference to Jesus.

young men. John asserts that the Christian life involves spiritual warfare. To be a Christian does not merely entail the enjoyment of sins forgiven and a warm relationship with God. It is also a vigorous battle against evil.

overcome. "Overcoming" is an important theme in all of John's writing (see John 16:33; 1 John 4:4; 5:4–5; Rev. 2:7ff). In the same way that Christ overcame Satan via his death and resurrection, so too Christians are to overcome the evil one. Twice the "young men" are commended for showing themselves to be spiritually strong enough to have overcome Satan (vv. 13–14).

the evil one. Satan, the ruler of darkness (see vv. 8–11) and the source of evil.

2:14 word of God. This is the source of the overcoming power displayed by the "young men." They know God's will and have lived in conformity to it.

lives in you. The word of God is meant not only to be understood, but it is also intended to be incorporated into a person's very being.

2:15–17 Having just assured his hearers about their secure relationship with God, John now finds it necessary to warn them about an attitude that could bring them down, lest they now feel immune to the power of evil. The attitude they are to avoid is "love of the world." John bases his command on two factors: the incompatibility of love for God with love for the world (vv. 15–16), and the transience of worldly desires in comparison to the everlasting life of those

who do God's will (v. 17). John is attacking an attitude (love of the world). He is not attacking "things" *per se*, much less people.

2:15 love. As in verse 5 and verse 10, the love which John speaks about is not so much an emotional response as it is the act of caring, expressed by what a person does. As such, this "love" is appropriately directed toward God (v. 5) and toward others (v. 10), but not toward the pleasures of the world.

world. The word John uses here is *kosmos* and in this context it means that which is alienated from God and is, in fact, contrary to who God is. It refers to pagan culture which has abandoned God. "Our author means human society insofar as it is organized on wrong principles and characterized by base desires, false values and egosim" (Dodd).

2:16 everything. Since God created the world (John 1:3), John cannot mean that everything in the world is automatically evil. In this verse, it is evident that what he had in mind is those aspects of the world which stand in opposition to God's ways.

cravings. That part of human nature which demands gratification—be it for sexual pleasure, for luxury, for possessions, for expensive food, for whatever.

lust of his eyes. Greed which is aroused by sight. A person sees something and wants it. (For examples of this, see Gen. 3:6; Josh. 7:21; 2 Sam. 11:2–4.)

boasting. Pride in one's possessions; an attitude of arrogance because one has acquired so much. In its original Greek usage, this word referred to a man who claimed to be important because he had achieved so much when, in fact, he really had done very little. These three attitudes are interconnected. "Selfish human desire is stimulated by what the eye sees and expresses itself in outward show" (Marshall). Taken together they add up to a materialistic view of the world.

2:17 pass away. To give oneself over to the love of the world is foolish because the world with its values and goods is already passing away (v. 8). Those who love the world will pass away with it, while those who love God will live forever.

lives forever. In contrast to those who live for the moment are those who give themselves to eternal, unchanging realities. Eternal life is one of God's gifts to the Christian.

UNIT 5—Warning Against Antichrists / 1 John 2:18-27

Warning Against Antichrists

[18]*Dear children, this is the last hour; and as you have heard that the antichrist is coming, even now many antichrists have come. This is how we know it is the last hour.* [19]*They went out from us, but they did not really belong to us. For if they had belonged to us, they would have remained with us; but their going showed that none of them belonged to us.*

[20]*But you have an anointing from the Holy One, and all of you know the truth.*[a] [21]*I do not write to you because you do not know the truth, but because you do know it and because no lie comes from the truth.* [22]*Who is the liar? It is the man who denies that Jesus is the Christ. Such a man is the antichrist—he denies the Father and* the Son. [23]*No one who denies the Son has the Father; whoever acknowledges the Son has the Father also.*

[24]*See that what you have heard from the beginning remains in you. If it does, you also will remain in the Son and in the Father.* [25]*And this is what he promised us—even eternal life.*

[26]*I am writing these things to you about those who are trying to lead you astray.* [27]*As for you, the anointing you received from him remains in you, and you do not need anyone to teach you. But as his anointing teaches you about all things and as that anointing is real, not counterfeit—just as it has taught you, remain in him.*

[a]20 Some manuscripts *and you know all things*

READ

First Reading / First Impressions: In this passage, John sounds like a:

❏ doomsday prophet ❏ parent giving lecture #101

❏ wise old owl speaking from experience ❏ leader angry at others who disagree with him

Second Reading / Big Idea: In your own words, how would you express what you think is the key verse or point here?

SEARCH

1. What is John referring to when he says, "This is the last hour ..." (v. 18; see note)?

2. From verses 19 and 22, how would you recognize an antichrist if you met one (see 4:3; 2 John 7)?

3. By contrast, what do these verses imply are the marks of a true Christian?

4. How would you explain what John means by the "anointing" (vv. 20,27; see notes)?

5. What does John mean in verse 23 by "acknowledging" the Son (see 1:3,7; 2:1–6; 4:2,15)?

6. In verse 27, does John mean they have no need of teachers at all (see note)? Why?

APPLY
Look for the "three tests" for a Christian that have been presented in this chapter, and jot down what you find for each test in your own words.

The Moral Test (1 John 2:3–6)

The Social Test (1 John 2:7–11)

The Doctrinal Test (1 John 2:18–27)

In which of these three areas do you see yourself as most vulnerable to the "evil one"? Why?

GROUP AGENDA

After the first part, read the Scripture out loud and divide into groups of 4. Then come back together for the third part.

TO BEGIN / 10–15 Min. (Choose 1 or 2)

1. How much of a problem did you have with lying when you were a kid? Can you remember a time when you got caught lying?

2. Who was your favorite teacher in high school?

3. Who has been like a spiritual parent to you—caring enough to warn you when necessary?

TO GO DEEPER / 30 Min. (Choose 2 or 3)

1. From studying this passage and reading the notes, what would you say was going on that prompted John to write this passage?

2. If you have done the homework, choose a question from READ or SEARCH to answer.

3. In what way are the antichrists in this passage foreshadowing the Antichrist to come? How do you see the "spirit of antichrist" at work today?

4. What criteria can you use to distinguish between new insights into Christian truths that the Holy Spirit brings to light, and new teachings that undermine Christian faith? What keeps a person from being led astray?

5. Why are there only two options in verse 23?

6. CASE STUDY: Your friend Rhonda tells you that she is really excited about Jesus, but wants nothing to do with the church. "The church is full of hypocrites who have nothing to teach me. Besides, I've got the Spirit now so who needs some minister telling me what I have to believe? My job is to spread Jesus' message, not to sit and listen to boring sermons." What could you share about the importance of remaining with the church from your own experience?

TO CLOSE / 15–30 Min.

1. Are you working on your mission as a group? Are you inviting new people to join you?

2. How did you answer APPLY, particularly the last question?

3. How do you sense the Holy Spirit's presence in your life? How do you need a greater sense of his presence?

4. How would you like the group to pray for you?

NOTES

Summary. Having assured the members of his church that they are walking in the Christian way, John returns to the question of how to distinguish between those who are true Christians and those who are counterfeit Christians. Thus far in his epistle he has defined two tests which enable one to make such a distinction: the true Christian is obedient to God's commands (the moral test, vv. 3–6) and the true Christian loves other people (the social test, vv. 7–11). Now he adds a third test: the true Christian remains firmly committed to the truth of God. This is the doctrinal test (Stott).

2:18 *the last hour.* The early Christians understood clearly that the first coming of Christ (the Incarnation) inaugurated "the last days." They also knew that his second coming (the *parousia*) would bring to a close the "last days" and usher in a new age in which God's rule would be visible and universal. In the first century the expectation was that this second coming of Jesus would take place in the immediate future. It could, in fact, happen at literally any moment. In this passage, one catches this sense of urgency. "The time is short," John is saying, "this is the last hour. He is coming back. So be ready." It is almost as if a clock is ticking away the final moments before the Second Coming.

antichrist. Although John is the only New Testament writer to use this term (see 2:22; 4:3; 2 John 7), the same concept is present in other parts of Scripture (e.g., Mark 13:22 and 2 Thess. 2:1–12), namely that one day an opponent to Christ will arise who is the incarnation of evil and Satan—just as Christ was the incarnation of good and God.

antichrists. John points out that the coming of the Antichrist was not just some future threat. Even at that moment the "spirit of the antichrist" (see 4:3) was loose in the world and active in those who deny Christ and his teachings (see v. 22).

2:19 *They went out from us.* John now identifies those who are imbued with the spirit of the antichrist. They are none other than the secessionists who left the church and even now seek to win over their former friends and colleagues to their point of view (see v. 26).

2:20 *an anointing.* In the Old Testament, when a king or a priest was consecrated to God's service, oil was poured on them as part of the ceremony. Here the noun refers to the *means* of anointing, namely the Holy Spirit. Just as Jesus was anointed with the Holy Spirit (Luke 4:18; Acts 10:38), so too is the believer. The Holy Spirit is thus the one that guides the Christian into all truth (John 14:17; 15:26; 16:13).

all of you. In contrast to the secessionists who claimed to have special, esoteric insight into spiritual truth not available to others (this was the source of their new doctrine), John assures his readers that *all* Christians know the truth, not just an elite few.

know the truth. The departure of the secessionists from the church was not the only evidence that "they did not really belong to us." The Christians already knew that they espoused false doctrines by virtue of their Holy Spirit derived insight into what was true.

2:22 John now reveals the master lie in the secessionists' false teaching; they deny that Jesus is the Messiah and the Son of God. This is an obvious lie that all true Christians will immediately recognize. "The antichrists probably taught (as some later Gnostics certainly taught) that Jesus was born and died a man, and that 'the Christ,' by which they meant a divine emanation, was within Him only during His public ministry, descending upon Him before the cross. They thus denied that Jesus was or is the Christ or the Son. They made Him a mere man invested for a brief period with divine powers or even adopted into the Godhead, but they denied that the man Jesus and the Eternal Son were and are the same Person, possessing two perfect natures, human and divine. In a word they denied the incarnation" (Stott).

2:23 The Father and the Son are inseparable. To deny the Son is to deny the Father (despite what might be claimed). Likewise, to confess the Son is to confess the Father (see John 10:30). This is the awful effect of the secessionists' heresy: to deny Jesus makes fellowship with God impossible.

denies / acknowledges. These are the only two options when it comes to Jesus. The idea here is of public confession and public denial (see Matt. 10:32–33; John 12:42; Rom. 10:9–10).

2:24–27 "Here, then, are the two main safeguards against error—the apostolic Word and the anointing Spirit. Both are received at conversion. 'You have heard' the Word (v. 24) he says, and 'you received' (v. 27) the Spirit, although, indeed, he implies, the Word has come to you from us (1:2,3,5), while you have received the Spirit direct *of*, that is from, *him*, 'the Holy One' (vv. 20,27). The Word is an objective safeguard, while the anointing of the Spirit is a sub-

jective experience; but both the apostolic teaching and the Heavenly Teacher are necessary for continuance in the truth. And both are to be personally and inwardly grasped" (Stott).

2:24 *See that.* John now issues a command. In the face of the lies of the antichrists they are to remain faithful to the Word of God.

what you have heard from the beginning. As an antidote to heresy, John urges his readers to let the original message which they heard right from the start of their Christian lives control their perspective. By urging them to remain faithful to the original apostolic word preached to them, he is ruling out private revelation that would deny or contradict this message—revelation such as the secessionists' new doctrines.

remain. John's point is that when they remain in the truth they will remain in fellowship with God. To remain "expresses a continuing relationship. It is not enough merely to have heard and assented to the message in time past. The message must continue to be present and active in the lives of those who have heard it. They must continually call it to mind and let it affect their lives" (Marshall).

2:25 *eternal life.* What has been promised the Christian is the sharing of the very life of God—both now in the present (beginning at conversion) and on into the future after death (John 3:36; 6:40,47; 17:3).

2:26 *lead you astray.* John now reveals more about the secessionists. They were not simply content to leave the church and form their own fellowship based on their private doctrines. Instead, they actively sought to make converts from among the Christian community.

2:27 The ultimate safeguard against heresy is the Word of God which has been conveyed to their hearts by the Spirit with whom they have been anointed (Marshall).

remains in you. By God's grace, Christians remain faithful to the Word of God. Human response and divine activity are both part of the Christian life.

teach. John is not saying that after anointing by the Holy Spirit Christians need no more instruction. John, in fact, is instructing them via this letter! There are no "new" truths they need to learn besides what the apostles taught, and they certainly don't need any instruction by the false teachers.

UNIT 6—Children of God / 1 John 2:28–3:10

Children of God

²⁸*And now, dear children, continue in him, so that when he appears we may be confident and unashamed before him at his coming.*

²⁹*If you know that he is righteous, you know that everyone who does what is right has been born of him.*

3 *How great is the love the Father has lavished on us, that we should be called children of God! And that is what we are! The reason the world does not know us is that it did not know him. ²Dear friends, now we are children of God, and what we will be has not yet been made known. But we know that when he appears,ª we shall be like him, for we shall see him as he is. ³Everyone who has this hope in him purifies himself, just as he is pure.*

⁴*Everyone who sins breaks the law; in fact, sin is lawlessness. ⁵But you know that he appeared so that he might take away our sins.*

And in him is no sin. ⁶No one who lives in him keeps on sinning. No one who continues to sin has either seen him or known him.

⁷*Dear children, do not let anyone lead you astray. He who does what is right is righteous, just as he is righteous. ⁸He who does what is sinful is of the devil, because the devil has been sinning from the beginning. The reason the Son of God appeared was to destroy the devil's work. ⁹No one who is born of God will continue to sin, because God's seed remains in him; he cannot go on sinning, because he has been born of God. ¹⁰This is how we know who the children of God are and who the children of the devil are: Anyone who does not do what is right is not a child of God; nor is anyone who does not love his brother.*

ª2 Or *when it is made known*

READ

First Reading / First Impressions: What old proverb best catches the idea of this passage?

❏ Like father, like son. ❏ Birds of a feather flock together.

❏ One rotten apple spoils the barrel. ❏ You can tell a man's character by the company he keeps.

Second Reading / Big Idea: What are some earlier passages in 1 John that remind you of this section?

SEARCH

1. What do verses 3:1–2 imply about God? What does this mean for your self-image?

2. In 3:6 and 3:9, does John mean a Christian cannot sin (see notes)? How do these verses fit with 1:8?

3. From what John writes here, what error do you think the false teachers were teaching?

Leadership Training Supplement

YOU ARE
HERE

BIRTH	GROWTH	RELEASE
101	201	301

What is the game plan for your group in the 301 stage?

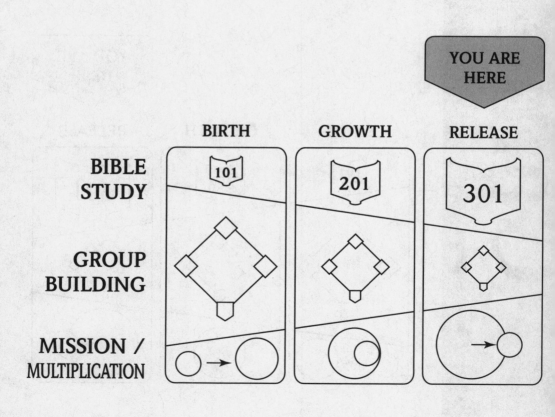

YOU ARE HERE

	BIRTH	GROWTH	RELEASE
BIBLE STUDY	101	201	301
GROUP BUILDING			
MISSION / MULTIPLICATION			

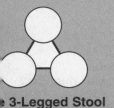

3-Legged Stool

The three essentials in a healthy small group are Bible Study, Group Building, and Mission / Multiplication. You need all three to stay balanced—like a 3-legged stool.

- To focus only on Bible Study will lead to scholasticism.
- To focus only on Group Building will lead to narcissism.
- To focus only on Mission will lead to burnout.

You need a game plan for the life cycle of the group where all of these elements are present in a purpose-driven strategy.

Bible Study

To develop the habit and skills for personal Bible Study.

TWO LEVELS: (1) Personal—on your own, and (2) Group study with your small group. In the personal Bible Study, you will be introduced to skills for reflection, self-inventory, creative writing and journaling.

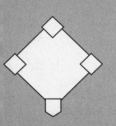

Group Building

To move into discipleship with group accountability, shared leadership and depth community.

At the close of this course, the group building aspect will reach its goal with a "going-away" party. If there are other groups in the church in this program, the event would be for all groups. Otherwise, the group will have its own closing celebration and commissioning time.

Mission / Multiplication

To commission the members of the leadership team from your group who are going to start a new group.

This Leadership Training Supplement is about your mission project. In six steps, your group will be led through a decision-making process to discover the leadership team within your group to form a new group.

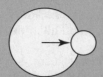

Mission / Multiplication

Where are you in the 3-stage life cycle of your mission?

You can't sit on a one-legged stool—or even a two-legged stool. It takes all three. A Bible Study and Care Group that doesn't have a MISSION will fall.

Birthing Cycle

The mission is to give birth to a new group at the conclusion of this course. In this 301 course, you are supposed to be at stage three. If you are not at stage three, you can still reach the mission goal if you stay focused.

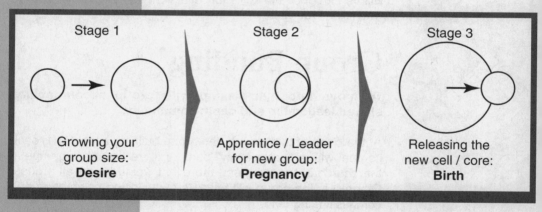

Stage 1	Stage 2	Stage 3
Growing your group size: **Desire**	Apprentice / Leader for new group: **Pregnancy**	Releasing the new cell / core: **Birth**

The birthing process begins with DESIRE. If you do not want to birth a new group, it will never happen. Desire keeps the group focused on inviting new people into your group every week—until your group grows to about 10 or 12 people.

The second stage is PREGNANCY. By recognizing the gifts of people in your group, you are able to designate two or three people who will ultimately be the missionaries in your group to form a new group. This is called the "leadership core."

The third stage is BIRTH—which takes place at the end of this course, when the whole group commissions the core or cell to move out and start the new group.

6 Steps to Birth a Group

Step 1

Desire

Is your group purpose-driven about mission?

Take this pop quiz and see how purpose-driven you are. Then, study the "four fallacies" about groups.

Step 2

Assessment

Is your church purpose-driven about groups?

Pinpoint where you are coming from and where most of the people in small groups in your church come from.

Step 3

Survey

Where's the itch for those in your church who are not involved in groups?

Take this churchwide survey to discover the felt needs of those in your church who do not seem to be interested in small groups.

Step 4

Brainstorming

What did you learn about your church from the survey?

Debrief the survey in the previous step to decide how your small group could make a difference in starting a new group.

Step 5

Barnstorming

Who are you going to invite?

Build a prospect list of people you think might be interested in joining a new group.

Step 6

Commissioning

Congratulations. You deserve a party.

Commission the leadership core from your group who are going to be your missionaries to start a new group. Then, for the rest of the "mother group," work on your covenant for starting over ... with a few empty chairs.

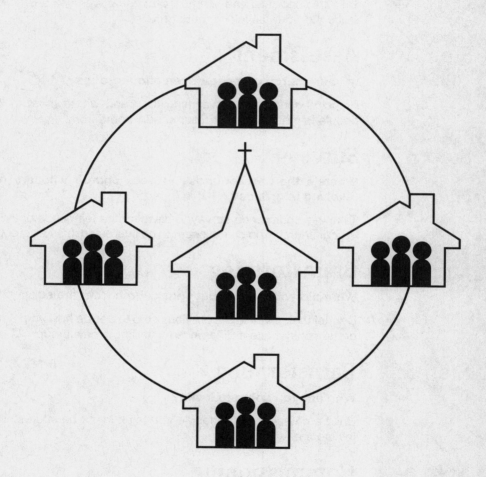

Step 1

Desire

Is your group purpose-driven about mission?

The greatest danger to any chain is its strongest link. This is especially true of Bible Study groups. The very depth of the study keeps new people from joining, or feeling comfortable when they join. In the end the group grows inward, becoming self-centered and spiritually insensitive.

To prevent this from happening in your group, take this pop quiz and share the results with your group.

	Yes	No
1. Are you a committed follower of Jesus Christ?	❐	❐
2. Do you believe that Jesus Christ wants you to share your faith with others?	❐	❐
3. Do you believe that every Christian needs to belong to a small, caring community where Jesus Christ is affirmed?	❐	❐
4. Do you know of people in your church who are not presently involved in a small group?	❐	❐
5. Do you know friends on the fringe of the church who need to belong to a life-sharing small group?	❐	❐
6. Do you believe that God has a will and plan for your life?	❐	❐
7. Are you willing to be open to what God might do through you in this small group?	❐	❐
8. Are you open to the possibility that God might use you to form a new group?	❐	❐

If you can't say "No" to any of these questions, consider yourself committed!

What Is a Small Group?

A Small Group is an intentional, face-to-face gathering of people in a similar stage of life at a regular time with a common purpose of discovering and growing in a relationship with Jesus Christ.

Small Groups are the disciple-making strategy of Flamingo Road Church. The behaviors of the 12 step strategy are the goals we want to achieve with each individual in small group. These goals are accomplished through a new members class (membership) and continues in a regular on-going small group (maturity, ministry and multiplication).

Keys to an Effective Small Group Ministry

1. Care for all people (members/guests) through organized active Care Groups.
2. Teach the Bible interactively while making life application.
3. Build a Servant Leadership Team.
4. Birth New Groups.

Commitments of all Small Group Leaders are ...

... all the behaviors represented in the 12 step strategy
... to lead their group to be an effective small group as mentioned above.
... use curriculum approved by small group pastor

Taken from the Small Group Training Manual of Flamingo Road Community Church, Fort Lauderdale, FL.

Four Fallacies About Small Groups

Are you suffering from one of these four misconceptions when it comes to small groups? Check yourself on these fallacies.

Fallacy #1: It takes 10 to 12 people to start a small group.

Wrong. The best size to start with is three or four people—which leaves room in the group for growth. Start "small" and pray that God will fill the "empty chair" ... and watch it happen.

Fallacy #2: It takes a lot of skill to lead a small group.

Wrong again. Sticking to the three-part tight agenda makes it possible for nearly anyone to lead a group. For certain support and recovery groups more skills are required, but the typical Bible Study and Care Group can be led by anyone with lots of heart and vision.

Fallacy #3: To assure confidentiality, the "door" should be closed after the first session.

For certain "high risk" groups this is true; but for the average Bible Study and Care Group all you need is the rule that "nothing that is said in the group is discussed outside of the group."

Fallacy #4: The longer the group lasts, the better it gets.

Not necessarily. The bell curve for effective small groups usually peaks in the second year. Unless new life is brought into the group, the group will decline in vitality. It is better to release the group (and become a reunion group) when it is at its peak than to run the risk of burnout.

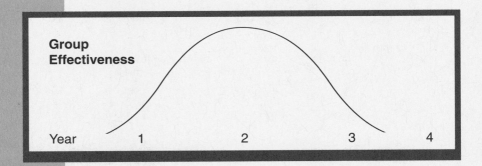

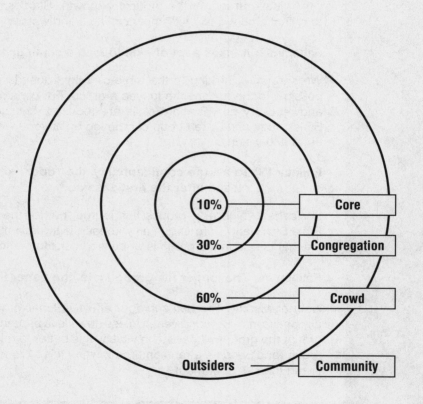

Assessment

Is your church purpose-driven about groups?

Most of the people who come to small groups in the church are from the highly committed CORE of the church. How about your group?

Pinpoint Your Group

The graph on the opposite page represents the four types of people typically found in your church and in your community.

- **10% Core:** The "spiritual core" of the church and the church leadership.

- **30% Congregation:** Those who come to church regularly and are faithful in giving.

- **60% Crowd:** Those on the membership roles who attend only twice a year. They have fallen through the cracks.

- **Outside Community:** Those who live in the surrounding area but do not belong to any church.

Step 1: On the opposite page, put a series of dots in the appropriate circles where the members of your group come from.

Step 2: If you know of other small groups in your church, put some more dots on the graph to represent the people in those groups. When you are finished, stop and ask your group this question:

"Why do the groups in our church appeal only to the people who are represented by the dots on this graph?"

Four Kinds of Small Groups

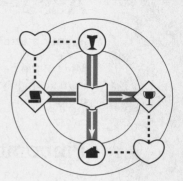

SUPPORT / RECOVERY GROUPS
- Felt needs
- Short-term
- Low-level commitment
- Seeker Bible Study

These groups are designed to appeal to hurting people on the fringe of the church and in the community.

PULPIT-BASED GROUPS
- Around the Scripture in the Sunday lesson
- With handout in Sunday bulletin
- With discussion questions
- No homework

These groups are designed to appeal to those who come to church and listen to the sermon but do not want to do homework.

DISCIPLESHIP / DEPTH BIBLE STUDY GROUPS
- Year-long commitment
- Depth Bible Study
- Homework required
- Curriculum based

These groups are designed to appeal to the 10% highly committed core of the church who are ready for discipleship.

COVENANT GROUPS
- Three-stage life cycle
- Renewal option
- Begins with 7-week contract
- Graded levels of Bible Study: 101, 201 and 301

Church Evaluation

You do NOT have to complete this assessment if you are not in the leadership core of your church, but it would be extremely valuable if your group does have members in the leadership core of your church.

1. Currently, what percentage of your church members are involved in small groups?

2. What kind of small groups are you offering in your church? (Study the four kinds of groups on the opposite page.)
   ❏ Support / Recovery Groups
   ❏ Pulpit-Based Groups
   ❏ Discipleship / Depth Bible Study Groups
   ❏ Three-stage Covenant Groups

3. Which statement below represents the position of your church on small groups?
   ❏ "Small Groups have never been on the drawing board at our church."
   ❏ "We have had small groups, but they fizzled."
   ❏ "Our church leadership has had negative experiences with small groups."
   ❏ "Small groups are the hope for our future."
   ❏ "We have Sunday school; that's plenty."

4. How would you describe the people who usually get involved in small groups?
   ❏ 10% Core   ❏ 30% Congregation   ❏ 60% Crowd

Risk and Supervision
This depends on the risk level of the group—the higher the risk, the higher the supervision. For the typical Bible Study group ⬜, pulpit-based group (Y), or covenant group ◈ (where there is little risk), supervision is minimal. For some support groups ♡ and all recovery groups (⚡), training and supervision are required.

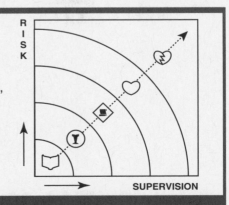

Step **3**

Survey

Where's the itch for those in your church who are not involved in groups?

This survey has been written for churchwide use—in hopes that you may be able to rewrite it and use it in your own church. The courses described in this survey are taken from the present Serendipity 101, 201 and 301 courses for small groups.

Churchwide Survey for Small Groups

Name_____Phone_____

Section 1: Interest in Shared-Experience Groups

A shared-experience group is short-term in nature (7–13 weeks) and brings people together based on a common interest, experience or need in their lives. The various topics being considered for shared-experience groups are listed below.

1. Which of these shared-experience courses might be of interest to you? Check all that apply in the grid below under question 1 (**Q1**).

2. Which of these shared-experience groups would you be interested in hosting or co-leading? Check all that apply in the grid below under question 2 (**Q2**).

3. Which of these shared-experience groups do you think would be of interest to a friend or relative of yours who is on the fringe of the church? Check all that apply in the grid below under question 3 (**Q3**).

101 **VIDEO Electives — 7–13 weeks: Sunday School with Groups**

	Q1	Q2	Q3
1. Dealing With Grief & Loss (Hope in the Midst of Pain)	☐	☐	☐
2. Divorce Recovery (Picking Up the Pieces)	☐	☐	☐
3. Marriage Enrichment (Making a Good Marriage Better)	☐	☐	☐
4. Parenting Adolescents (Easing the Way to Adulthood)	☐	☐	☐
5. Healthy Relationships (Living Within Defined Boundaries)	☐	☐	☐
6. Stress Management (Finding the Balance)	☐	☐	☐
7. 12 Steps (The Path to Wholeness)	☐	☐	☐

[101] BEGINNER Bible Study — 7- to 13-week groups

	Q1	Q2	Q3
8. Stressed Out (Keeping Your Cool)	☐	☐	☐
9. Core Values (Setting My Moral Compass)	☐	☐	☐
10. Marriage (Seasons of Growth)	☐	☐	☐
11. Jesus (Up Close & Personal)	☐	☐	☐
12. Gifts & Calling (Discovering God's Will)	☐	☐	☐
13. Relationships (Learning to Love)	☐	☐	☐
14. Assessment (Personal Audit)	☐	☐	☐
15. Family (Stages of Parenting)	☐	☐	☐
16. Wholeness (Time for a Checkup)	☐	☐	☐
17. Beliefs (Basic Christianity)	☐	☐	☐

[201] DEEPER Bible Study — Varying Length Courses

	Q1	Q2	Q3
18. Supernatural: Amazing Stories (Jesus' Miracles) 13 wks.	☐	☐	☐
19. Discipleship: In His Steps (Life of Christ) 13 wks.	☐	☐	☐
20. Wisdom: The Jesus Classics (Jesus' Parables) 13 wks.	☐	☐	☐
21. Challenge: Attitude Adjustment (Sermon on the Mount) 13 wks.	☐	☐	☐
22. Endurance: Running the Race (Philippians) 11 wks.	☐	☐	☐
23. Teamwork: Together in Christ (Ephesians) 12 wks.	☐	☐	☐
24. Integrity: Taking on Tough Issues (1 Corinthians) 12–23 wks.	☐	☐	☐
25. Gospel: Jesus of Nazareth (Gospel of Mark) 13–26 wks.	☐	☐	☐
26. Leadership: Passing the Torch (1 & 2 Timothy) 14 wks.	☐	☐	☐
27. Excellence: Mastering the Basics (Romans) 15–27 wks.	☐	☐	☐
28. Hope: Looking at the End of Time (Revelation) 13–26 wks.	☐	☐	☐
29. Faithfulness: Walking in the Light (1 John) 11 wks.	☐	☐	☐
30. Freedom: Living by Grace (Galatians) 13 wks.	☐	☐	☐
31. Perseverance: Staying the Course (1 Peter) 10 wks.	☐	☐	☐
32. Performance: Faith at Work (James) 12 wks.	☐	☐	☐

[301] DEPTH Bible Study — 13-week groups

	Q1	Q2	Q3
33. Ephesians (Our Riches in Christ)	☐	☐	☐
34. James (Walking the Talk)	☐	☐	☐
35. Life of Christ (Behold the Man)	☐	☐	☐
36. Miracles (Signs and Wonders)	☐	☐	☐
37. Parables (Virtual Reality)	☐	☐	☐
38. Philippians (Joy Under Stress)	☐	☐	☐
39. Sermon on the Mount (Examining Your Life)	☐	☐	☐
40. 1 John (The Test of Faith)	☐	☐	☐

Section 2: Covenant Groups (Long-term)

A covenant group is longer term (like an extended family), starting with a commitment for 7–13 weeks, with an option of renewing your covenant for the rest of the year. A covenant group can decide to change the topics they study over time. The general themes for the covenant groups that our church is considering are listed on the previous two pages.

4. Which of the following long-term covenant groups would you be interested in?

   ❏ Singles   ❏ Men   ❏ Women

   ❏ Couples   ❏ Parents   ❏ Downtown

   ❏ Twenty-Something   ❏ Thirty-Something   ❏ Empty Nesters

   ❏ Mixed   ❏ Breakfast   ❏ Engineers

   ❏ Young Marrieds   ❏ Seniors   ❏ Sunday Brunch

Section 3: Pre-Covenant Groups (Short-term)

To give you a taste of a small group, our church is offering a 7-week "trial" program for groups. For this trial program, the group will use the course *Beginnings: A Taste of Serendipity.*

5. Would you be interested in joining a "trial" group?

   ❏ Yes   ❏ No   ❏ Maybe

6. What would be the most convenient time and place for you to meet?

   ❏ Weekday morning   ❏ At church

   ❏ Weekday evening   ❏ In a home

   ❏ Saturday morning

   ❏ Sunday after church

7. What kind of group would you prefer?

   ❏ Men

   ❏ Women

   ❏ Singles

   ❏ Couples

   ❏ Mixed

   ❏ Parents

   ❏ Seniors

   ❏ Around my age

   ❏ Doesn't matter

SERENDIPITY

BEGINNINGS

A TASTE OF SERENDIPITY

7 Sessions To Become
A Great Small Group!

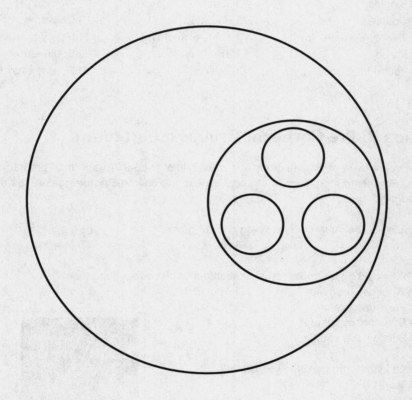

Step 4 Brainstorming

What did you learn about your church from the survey?

The Itch: Debrief together what you discovered from the survey about the need for small groups in your church. To begin with, find out in your group who checked Q3 for any of the 101 Video and 101 Beginner Electives (courses 1–17). Jot down in the box below the top three courses that you checked for 1–17.

Top Three Courses:

The Nitch: For the top three courses in the box above, find out if anyone in your group checked Q2 for these courses—i.e., that they would be willing to host or help lead a group that was interested in this course. Jot down the names of those in your group who checked Q2 in the box below.

Potential Hosts and Leaders:

The Apprentice / Leader and Leadership Core: Now, as a group, look over the names of the potential hosts and leaders you put in the box above and try to discern the person on this list who you think could easily be the leader of this new group, and one or two others who might fill out the Leadership Core for this new group. Jot down these names in the box below.

Apprentice / Leader and Leadership Core:

Leadership Training

Q&A

What is the purpose of Covenant Groups?*

The members of the Covenant Group come together for the purpose of helping each other to:

- *Love God with all their heart, soul, mind and strength (Mark 12:30).*
- *Love their neighbors as themselves (Mark 12:31).*
- *Make disciples (Matthew 28:19).*

What are the qualifications of a Covenant Group leader?

A Covenant Group leader functions as a lay pastor, taking on himself or herself the responsibility of providing the primary care for the members of the group. Therefore, a Covenant Group leader exemplifies the following characteristics:

- *believes in Jesus Christ as their Lord and Savior*
- *has been a Christian for a while*
- *continues to grow in their faith*
- *cares for the well-being of others*
- *is able to set goals and work toward them*
- *demonstrates moral integrity*
- *listens to others*
- *is empathetic*
- *is willing to learn from others*
- *demonstrates flexibility*
- *respects others*
- *senses a call to serve*

A Covenant Group leader is not a perfect person! He or she need not know everything about leading and caring for others. Skills valuable to the role of a leader will be taught throughout the year, and care for the leader will be provided on an ongoing basis through a coach.

A Covenant Group leader is not necessarily a teacher. It is far more important that the leader be able to shepherd and care for the others in the group. Teaching is often a shared responsibility among group members.

---

* These four pages (M20–M23) are taken from the Training Manual For Group Leaders at Zionsville Presbyterian Church, Zionsville, IN, and are used by permission.

What does the church expect of a Covenant Group leader?

Every leader is asked to agree to the terms of the leader's covenant. Covenant Group leaders are to attend the monthly STP (Sharing, Training and Prayer) meeting. This gathering is held for the purposes of training and supporting leaders. The meeting takes place on the third Tuesday of each month, from 6:45 p.m. to 8:30 p.m. The two main elements of the STP event concern communication. The first half of the evening is devoted to disseminating the vision. The second half of the meeting consists of leaders huddling with their coach and with each other for the purpose of learning from one another. If a leader is unable to attend this meeting for some significant reason, he or she is to arrange another time to meet with their coach.

Leaders are also to fill out the Group Leader's Summary after every group event. This one-page reporting form takes only 10 minutes or so to complete and is a vital communication link between the staff liaison, the coach and the leader.

What can a Covenant Group leader expect in the way of support from the church?

A Covenant Group leader can expect the session and the staff to hold to the terms laid out in the Church's Covenant.

Every leader will be given a coach. This coach is someone whose ministry is to care for up to five leaders. The coach is charged with the responsibility of resourcing, encouraging, supporting, evaluating, challenging, loving and listening to the leaders in his or her care.

Every coach is supported by a staff member. If leaders ever have a situation where they feel that their coach is unable to help them, the staff liaison is there to be of assistance.

What is the role of a Covenant Group leader?

When people come together in groups, the group itself becomes an entity that is greater than the sum of its parts. The Covenant Group leader watches over the life and health of this new entity.

Leadership Training

Specifically the Covenant Group leader is to:

- *find an apprentice*
- *pray and prepare for group meetings*
- *notify their coach or staff of acute crisis conditions requiring response*
- *develop and maintain an atmosphere in which members of the group can discover and develop God-given spiritual gifts*
- *pray for the spiritual growth and protection of each member*
- *refer counseling cases that exceed experience level*
- *convene the group two to four times each month*
- *recruit a host/hostess, when appropriate, and to see that child care and refreshments are available and a venue is arranged*
- *develop a healthy balance of love, learn, do, decide*
- *assure God's redemptive agenda via Scripture, sharing, prayers, songs and worship*
- *assist the group in refraining from divisiveness or teachings contrary to church position*
- *accept responsibility for group growth through the open-chair strategy*
- *lead an exemplary life*
- *regularly touch base with members outside the context of the group meeting just to say "Hi" and to see how they are doing*
- *help the group form a covenant and to review the covenant periodically*

While the Covenant Group leader takes primary responsibility for these activities, he or she should involve members of the group in many of them.

Does a Covenant Group really have to have a leader?

Yes! Without a leader a Covenant Group is like a ship at sea with no captain. A ship without a captain is at the mercy of the prevailing current and is unable to prepare for what may lie ahead. However, a ship with a captain has her course mapped out, and there is always someone at the helm ready to respond if necessary. So it is with a Covenant Group. The leader serves the others in the group by working to chart the best course as they together pursue being God's people on earth.

Questions & Answers

What are the critical elements of a Covenant Group?

A Covenant Group needs to have:

- *a leader*
- *an apprentice / leader*
- *members*
- *an open chair*
- *a covenant (see page M32)*

What is an Apprentice / Leader and how do we find one?

An apprentice / leader is someone who agrees that in time he or she will step out into leadership. Historically churches have tended to ask only those who aggressively step forward to serve in leadership positions. Rarely have churches worked at developing leaders. The result has been that most churches experience the phenomenon where only 20% of the congregation does 80% of the work. This historical approach stifles the giftedness of 80% of the church's population! In addition, the church has burned out many of their stand-out leaders by asking them to lead too many programs and too many people. Without some form of apprentice / leadership development, the church is constrained to overload its highly motivated, "here-I-am-send-me" leaders. The apprentice / leader model is meant to address these concerns.

The apprentice / leader is not an assistant. An assistant seldom has plans of stepping into the leader's shoes. Instead, the apprentice / leader works alongside the leader, with the intent of one day becoming a leader themselves. Along the way he or she is experiencing on-the-job training, learning the skills necessary to serve a small group as its leader.

It is the responsibility of the leader to find an apprentice / leader. The most important tools for the leader in this process are prayer and observation. The leader should pray, asking God to send someone whom he or she could mentor and train as a leader. Accompanying these prayers should be efforts to observe those who demonstrate signs of giftedness in shepherding, organizing, listening and faith. The one who is on time and who routinely prepares diligently for the group could be a candidate. The leader could also begin using the time before and after worship services, as well as various fellowship and educational events, to meet others in the congregation. As relationships are established, and the extent of a leader's acquaintances are broadened, the opportunity for finding a suitable apprentice / leader increases.

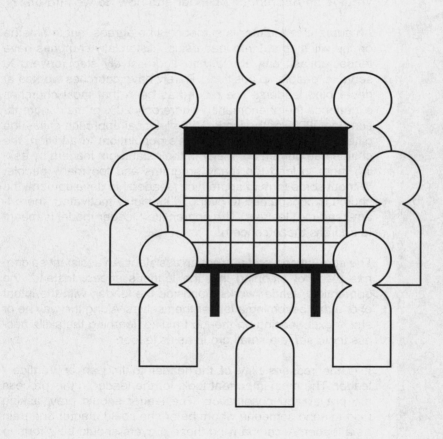

Step 5 Barnstorming

Who are you going to invite?

In the previous step, you identified the Apprentice / Leader and one or two others in your group who are going to be the leadership cell or core to start a new group.

Now, as a whole group, spend a few minutes creating a prospect list of people you would like to invite into this new group. Ask someone in your group to be the secretary and write down in the boxes below the names of people who come to mind:

Friends: Who are your friends in the church who you think might be interested in a small group?

Affinity: What are the special interests of the people in your leadership cell and who are the people in your church with the same interests? For instance, if the people in your leadership cell love tennis, who are the people in your church who might be interested in a small group before tennis? What about book lovers, entrepreneurs, empty nesters, senior citizens, stock watchers, etc.?

How Serendipity 101 Courses Make Leading A Beginner Group Easy:

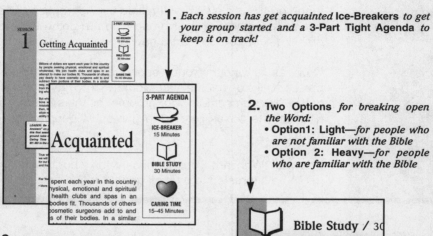

1. *Each session has get acquainted* **Ice-Breakers** *to get your group started and a* **3-Part Tight Agenda** *to keep it on track!*

2. **Two Options** *for breaking open the Word:*
- **Option1: Light**—*for people who are not familiar with the Bible*
- **Option 2: Heavy**—*for people who are familiar with the Bible*

3. **Study Helps** *for the Group Leader include Margin Tips, Reference Notes and Guided Questionnaires for Bible Study.*

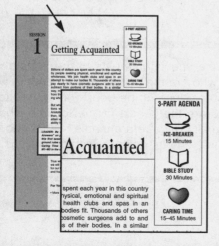

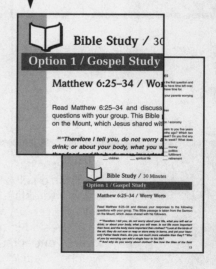

Felt Needs: Who are the people you know with the same felt needs? These people might be on the fringe of the church or even outside of the church. Go back to the survey on pages M15–M16 (the 101 courses) and think of people you feel could be hot prospects. For instance, who would be interested in "Stressed Out," "Marriage," "Wholeness," "Healthy Relationships," "Parenting Adolescents," etc.?

Geographical Location: Where do the people in your leadership team live or work, and who are the people in your church in the same area?

The Four Circles: Now, on this diagram, pinpoint the people you have jotted down in the four circles. Do you have any people on this list from the **Crowd** (the church dropouts)? Do you have anyone on your list from the **Community** (who do not attend any church)? It's really important that you have people from all four circles on your list.

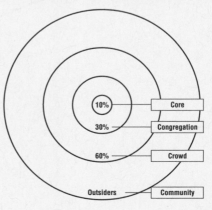

M27

Step 6 Commissioning

Congratulations. You deserve a party.

Only two things remain for you to decide: (1) How are you going to commission the leadership team for the new group and (2) What is the rest of your group going to do next?

Going-away party

You have several options. If the church is planning a church-wide event for all of the groups (such as a graduation banquet), you would have a table at this event for your group. If your church is not planning an event, you must plan your own going-away party.

At this party, you may want to reminisce about your life together as a group, have fun making some "Wild Predictions," share a Bible Study time, and conclude with a time of commissioning and prayer.

Reminiscing Questions

1. What do you remember about the first time you attended this group?

2. How did you feel about opening up in this group and sharing your story?

3. What was the funniest thing that happened in this group?

4. What was the high point for you in this group?

5. What will you miss most about this group?

6. How would you like this group to stay in touch with each other after you multiply?

7. How did this group contribute to your life?

8. What is the biggest change that has occurred in your life since joining this group?

Wild Predictions

Try to match the people in your group to the crazy forecasts below. (Don't take it too seriously; it's meant to be fun!) Read out loud the first item and ask everyone to call out the name of the person who is most likely to accomplish this feat. Then, read the next item and ask everyone to make a new prediction, etc.

THE PERSON IN OUR GROUP MOST LIKELY TO ...

Be the used-car salesperson of the year

Replace Regis Philbin on *Regis and Kathie Lee*

Replace Vanna White on *Wheel of Fortune*

Rollerblade across the country

Open a charm school for Harley-Davidson bikers

Discover a new use for underarm deodorant

Run a dating service for lonely singles

Rise to the top in the CIA

Appear on the cover of *Muscle & Fitness Magazine*

Win the Iditarod dogsled race in Alaska

Make a fortune on pay toilet rentals

Write a best-selling novel based on their love life

Get listed in the *Guinness Book of World Records* for marathon dancing

Win the blue ribbon at the state fair for best Rocky Mountain oyster recipe

Bungee jump off the Golden Gate Bridge

Be the first woman to win the Indianapolis 500

Win the *MAD Magazine* award for worst jokes

Reflection Bible Study

Barnabas and Saul Sent Off — Acts 13:1–3, NIV

13 *In the church at Antioch there were prophets and teachers: Barnabas, Simeon called Niger, Lucius of Cyrene, Manaen (who had been brought up with Herod the tetrarch) and Saul. ²While they were worshiping the Lord and fasting, the Holy Spirit said, "Set apart for me Barnabas and Saul for the work to which I have called them." ³So after they had fasted and prayed, they placed their hands on them and sent them off.*

1. Why do you think God chose this small group in Antioch to launch the first missionary journey (instead of the church headquarters in Jerusalem)?
   ❒ It was merely coincidental.
   ❒ They were following the leading of the Holy Spirit.
   ❒ They were a bunch of outcasts from the fringe of the church.
   ❒ They didn't know how to "paint inside the lines."

2. How do you think the leadership back in Jerusalem felt when they heard what these guys were doing?
   ❒ thrilled   ❒ angry that they didn't follow protocol
   ❒ embarrassed   ❒ They probably didn't hear about it until later.

3. Why do you think the small group chose two people to send out instead of one?
   ❒ for companionship
   ❒ They had different gifts: Paul was a hothead, Barnabas an encourager.
   ❒ It was coincidental.

4. As you think about sending out some members of your small group to give "birth" to a new group, what is your greatest concern for these people?
   ❒ keeping the faith   ❒ keeping their personal walk with Christ
   ❒ keeping the vision   ❒ keeping in touch with us for support

5. As one who is going to lead or colead a new group, how would you describe your emotions right now?
   ❒ a nervous wreck   ❒ delivery room jitters
   ❒ pregnant with excitement   ❒ Ask me next week.

6. If you could say one word of encouragement to those who are going to be new leaders, what would it be?
   ❒ I'll be praying for you.   ❒ You can do it.
   ❒ Call me anytime.   ❒ It's okay to fail.

What do we do next?

For those who are going to stay with the "mother group," you need to decide on your new covenant and who you are going to invite to fill the empty chairs left by the departing "missionaries."

Do we ever meet again?

Definitely! Plan NOW for "homecoming" next year when the new group returns for a time of celebration. Four good times: the World Series, Super Bowl, Final Four and Stanley Cup.

Group Covenant

Any group can benefit from creating or renewing a group covenant. Take some time for those remaining in the "mother group" to discuss the following questions. When everyone in the group has the same expectations for the group, everything runs more smoothly.

1. The purpose of our group is:

2. The goals of our group are:

3. We will meet for _____ weeks, after which we will decide if we wish to continue as a group. If we do decide to continue, we will reconsider this covenant.

4. We will meet _____ (weekly, every other week, monthly).

5. Our meetings will be from _____ o'clock to _____ o'clock, and we will strive to start and end on time.

6. We will meet at _____ or rotate from house to house.

7. We will take care of the following details:　　❒ child care　　❒ refreshments

8. We agree to the following rules for our group:

   ❒ PRIORITY: While we are in this group, group meetings have priority.

   ❒ PARTICIPATION: Everyone is given the right to their own opinion and all questions are respected.

   ❒ CONFIDENTIALITY: Anything said in the meeting is not to be repeated outside the meeting.

   ❒ EMPTY CHAIR: The group stays open to new people and invites prospective members to visit the group.

   ❒ SUPPORT: Permission is given to call each other in times of need.

   ❒ ADVICE GIVING: Unsolicited advice is not allowed.

   ❒ MISSION: We will do everything in our power to start a new group.

4. What characteristics of a person "born of God" are found in this passage?

5. What do the following verses indicate about the motives and reasons for living a holy life?

(2:28)

(2:29)

(3:1–3)

(3:6)

(3:9)

APPLY
Of the motives identified in the last SEARCH question, which one most spurs you on? Why?

Rate yourself on the following issues raised in this passage by putting an **"X"** somewhere on the spectrums.

IF JESUS WERE TO RETURN TONIGHT, I WOULD FEEL:

confident and unashamed (2:28)   fearful and ashamed

IN MY LIFE, SIN IS THE:

exception   rule

WHEN IT COMES TO LOVING MY "BROTHERS AND SISTERS," I LIVE LIKE:

a child of God (3:10)   a child of the devil (3:10)

GROUP AGENDA

After the first part, read the Scripture out loud and divide into groups of 4. Then come back together for the third part.

TO BEGIN / 10–15 Min. (Choose 1 or 2)

1. Whose coming would motivate you to get busy and clean house: Your boss? Your inlaws? Your small group?

2. When you were a child, were you more motivated to obey your parents by threats or promises?

3. What is one of your parents' characteristics that you definitely have inherited?

TO GO DEEPER / 30 Min. (Choose 2 or 3)

1. From studying this passage and the reference notes, what false teaching do you think John is combatting? Is John saying true Christians don't sin? If not, what *is* he saying?

2. How can a Christian recognize and deal with our society's "whatever is right for you" attitude (moral relativism)?

3. As you get older, do you find the old sinful desires easier or harder to resist?

4. How does it make you feel to know that followers of Christ one day "shall be like him"?

5. How have you experienced God's lavish love lately?

6. CASE STUDY: Joe became a Christian about a month ago. He was quite the "party animal" before. Sexually active. Fast living. Heavy drinking. Suddenly, his whole life has started to change. His old friends are mystified. "Joe has got religion," they say, "but it won't last." Joe is discouraged by this ridicule, and wonders if his friends are probably right. How would you encourage him?

TO CLOSE / 15–30 Min.

1. Are you thinking and dreaming about your group's mission? (See the center section.)

2. Share your answers to APPLY.

3. How clearly has your life mirrored God this week: Like a clear mountain lake? Like a rushing stream with occasional pools? Like pounding waves—not much space for God to be seen? Why?

4. How can the group pray for you?

NOTES

Summary. In the previous unit (2:18–27), John articulated the third and final test that distinguishes a cult from a Christian church. In the next three units (found in 2:28 to 4:6), he will go back over these three tests a second time. In this unit (2:28–3:10), he reexamines the moral test by discussing obedience once again. In the next unit (3:11–24), he reexamines the social test by discussing once again what is involved in loving other people. In the third unit (4:1–6), he reexamines the doctrinal test by pointing out again the correct view of Jesus.

2:28–3:3 Previously, John urged his readers to resist the proselytizing of the dissenters and to remain in Christ. In these verses he continues to urge his readers to remain in Christ, but now the reason he gives has to do with the second coming of Christ. If they remain in Christ, when they meet the Lord at the Second Coming they will not be ashamed. Instead, they will be confident before the Lord (2:28). Furthermore, they know that they will see Christ as he is and be made like him (3:2). The Second Coming is thus a source of great hope for the Christian and an encouragement to holy living (3:3).

2:28 *continue.* The word translated here as "continue" is the same Greek word that was translated "remain" in 2:19,24,27. It can be translated in a variety of ways: "to abide," "to remain steadfast," "to dwell," "to rest," "to persist," "to persevere," or "to be intimately united to." However, the best rendering is "to remain" or "to abide in."

confident and unashamed. On the Day of Judgment (which will occur at the Second Coming) those who have rejected Christ will feel a sense of unworthiness and shame in the presence of his holiness (Isa. 6:5), and because of their open disgrace at having rejected Christ. In contrast, Christians will be able boldly to approach the royal presence because they have lived their lives in union with Christ.

2:29 *born of him.* Christians are those who experience "spiritual rebirth." John thus defines the relationship between the believer and God by means of the analogy of the relationship between a child and a father (see also Titus 3:5; 1 Peter 1:3,23). One consequence of spiritual rebirth is right living. It is, in fact, a sign of rebirth as the child begins to display the characteristics of his or her Heavenly Father.

3:1 The precise nature of what Christians will become when they meet Christ is not fully clear ("what we will be has not yet been made known"). Yet they can get an idea of what they will be like by looking at Jesus ("we shall be like him"). In some way, Christians will become like Jesus when the process of glorification—which began at rebirth—is completed at the Second Coming.

3:3 *this hope.* Namely, that one day Christ will appear again at which time they will see him as he really is and be changed so as to become like him.

pure. This is a common word in the Bible denoting the outward purity required of those persons or objects involved in temple worship. In the usage here it speaks of the moral purity (freedom from sinning) that is required of Christians. Such purification is necessary for those who are in union with Christ. The secessionists, in contrast, were not much concerned about sin (1:5–2:2).

3:4–10 Having stated that those who are Christians have the hope of the Second Coming as their motivation for purifying themselves, John next looks at the sin from which they must purify themselves. In these verses he addresses the negative: the children of God must not sin. In 3:11–24 he will address the positive: instead, the children of God are to love one another.

3:5 John gives yet another reason for not sinning. The very purpose for Jesus to come in the first place was to take away sin. So it is obvious that Jesus stands over against sin. Furthermore, there was no sin in Jesus' life. The implication is that those who are in union with Christ will reflect this same abhorrence of sin.

in him is no sin. John asserts that Jesus was sinless. His testimony is all the more powerful since this is not his main point. John is not trying to prove anything. He is simply stating what he knows to be true. And John was in a position to know whether Jesus was actually without sin because he lived with Jesus for some three years. Those who live with us know us best. Yet John says—after having seen Jesus in a variety of situations over a three-year period—that Jesus is *without sin.*

3:6 John appears to be saying here (and in vv. 8–10) that a Christian *cannot sin.* Yet in other passages, he points out that Christians can and do sin (e.g., 1:8,10; 2:1; 5:16). Some scholars feel that what John has in mind here is willful and deliberate sin (as against involuntary error). Other scholars stress the tense of the verb that John uses: a Christian does not *keep* on sinning. In other words, Christians do not habitually sin. Still other scholars

feel that what John does here is to point out the ideal. This is what would happen if a Christian abided constantly in Christ. In any case, "John is arguing the incongruity rather than the impossibility of sin in the Christian" (Stott).

3:7 *lead you astray.* The secessionists deny that there is any incompatibility between being a Christian and continuing in sin. In other words, they not only seek to lead Christians away from the truth (2:26), they also seem to lead them into an immoral lifestyle.

3:8–10 In these verses John restates what he has said in verses 4–7. This statement parallels his previous statement except that here the focus is on the origin of sin (it is of the devil) rather than on the nature of sin (it is breaking the Law).

3:8 *sinful.* In verse 4, sinfulness was described as lawbreaking. Here sin is linked with Satan who from the beginning has sinned.

of the devil. Just as Christians display their Father's nature by moral living, so too others demonstrate by their immoral lifestyles that Satan is really their father.

3:9 *God's seed.* John probably is referring either to the Word of God (see Luke 8:11; James 1:18; 1 Peter 1:23) or to the Holy Spirit (see John 3:6) or to both, by which the Christian is kept from sin. In any case, "seed" is a metaphor for the indwelling power of God which brings forth new life.

cannot go on sinning. In 1:8,10 and 2:1, John attacks those who deny that they are sinners in need of forgiveness (i.e., those who are blind to the fact of their sin). Yet here he seems to say that Christians cannot sin. Some scholars feel that in chapter one John was responding to one aspect of the pre-Gnostic heresy of the secessionists—i.e., their teaching that those who were spiritually enlightened were perfect. But here he is dealing with a second aspect of that heresy—i.e., the teaching that sin did not matter. To those holding the first view he declared the universality of sin (all are sinners). Here, in the face of the second error, he declares the incompatibility of sin with the Christian life.

3:10 John here spells out in clear, unequivocal terms the moral test, although he casts it in negative terms: a person "who does not do right is not a child of God." He also articulates the social test—in anticipation of the next unit—again in negative terms: a person is not a child of God "who does not love his brother."

UNIT 7—Love One Another / 1 John 3:11-24

Love One Another

11This is the message you heard from the beginning: We should love one another. 12Do not be like Cain, who belonged to the evil one and murdered his brother. And why did he murder him? Because his own actions were evil and his brother's were righteous. 13Do not be surprised, my brothers, if the world hates you. 14We know that we have passed from death to life, because we love our brothers. Anyone who does not love remains in death. 15Anyone who hates his brother is a murderer, and you know that no murderer has eternal life in him.

16This is how we know what love is: Jesus Christ laid down his life for us. And we ought to lay down our lives for our brothers. 17If anyone has material possessions and sees his brother in need but has no pity on him, how can the love of God be in him? 18Dear children, let us not love with words or tongue but with actions and in truth. 19This then is how we know that we belong to the truth, and how we set our hearts at rest in his presence 20whenever our hearts condemn us. For God is greater than our hearts, and he knows everything.

21Dear friends, if our hearts do not condemn us, we have confidence before God 22and receive from him anything we ask, because we obey his commands and do what pleases him. 23And this is his command: to believe in the name of his Son, Jesus Christ, and to love one another as he commanded us. 24Those who obey his commands live in him, and he in them. And this is how we know that he lives in us: We know it by the Spirit he gave us.

READ

First Reading / First Impressions: From this passage, it seems that love:

- ❏ will conquer all
- ❏ makes the world go around
- ❏ is all you need
- ❏ is the gift that keeps on giving
- ❏ is like a flower and you are its only seed

Second Reading / Big Idea: If you had to reduce this passage to a slogan to fit on a T-shirt, what would you write?

SEARCH

1. From verse 11 and 2:7 (also 2 John 5), what must be going on that John again reminds the readers of what they have heard "from the beginning"?

2. Read the story of Cain and Abel in Genesis 4:1–8. How does the motive that lay behind Cain's actions apply to the way "the world" may treat Christians (vv. 12–13; see notes)?

3. If a person claims to be a Christian and still behaves like Cain toward a Christian brother, what news does John give this person (vv. 14–15)?

4. In contrast to Cain, what stands out to you about what real love involves (vv. 16–18; see notes)?

5. In the practical case John uses, what is the general principle to be applied (v. 17)?

6. What are we assured of through loving others (vv. 14,18–20,24)?

7. How are answered prayers and obedience connected (vv. 21–22; see notes)?

8. Compare verse 23 with Galatians 5:6b. From these passages, how would you sum up what it means to be a Christian?

APPLY

What is one way you want to apply love "Jesus style" this week in your family, work or community?

Go back and read the passage again and try to rephrase it into a prayer—a very personal prayer. For example: *Dear God, help me to love_____ and to demonstrate love by _____.* (You won't be asked to share this prayer in the group meeting.)

GROUP AGENDA

After the first part, read the Scripture out loud and divide into groups of 4. Then come back together for the third part.

TO BEGIN / 10–15 Min. (Choose 1 or 2)

1. Who was your first "true love" growing up?

2. How do you know when someone *really* loves you?

3. When have you been in need and then blessed by someone's gift to you?

TO GO DEEPER / 30 Min. (Choose 2 or 3)

1. What do you think Christians in the first century were encountering from the non-Christian world? Reading between the lines in this passage, what kind of support do you think they were giving each other?

2. What is the heart of John's message here? If you've completed the homework, what question, reference note or insight stands out to you as an illustration of John's message?

3. Although we normally think of love in terms of personal relationships, how does the picture of love in verses 16–18 affect: Our involvement in social issues like racism or welfare reform? Our stance on political issues like human rights and aid to developing countries?

4. How will obedience affect what we pray for (vv. 21–22)? What area of your life do you need to examine regarding the link between obedience and that which you are praying for?

5. CASE STUDY: Jim has been out of work for several months. His unemployment insurance is gone and the bank has foreclosed on his house. His wife works part-time, but that income isn't enough. They are proud people and won't ask for help, but you know about their situation. What should you do?

TO CLOSE / 15–30 Min.

1. Are you happy with your group's progress on developng your mission?

2. Do you know of anyone in your Christian community who needs your help at the moment?

3. How did you answer the first question in APPLY?

4. How would you like the group to pray today?

NOTES

Summary. The final verse of the previous unit (3:10) links together the idea of righteousness (the subject of that unit) and the idea of love (the subject of this unit). In that verse John says: "Anyone who does not do what is right is not a child of God; nor is anyone who does not love his brother." By this statement John moves from the first test of orthodoxy (the moral test) to the second test (the social test), which he expounds in this unit. This unit has two parts to it. In part one (vv. 11–18), John states the second test: true Christians love one another. He demonstrates this first by the means of a negative example (Cain) and then by the means of a positive example (Jesus). Part two (vv. 19–24) is a parenthesis in the flow of his thought in which he comments on assurance and on obedience, both in the context of prayer.

3:11 *you heard from the beginning.* Once again (as in 2:7,24) John reminds his readers that it was the teaching of the apostles that initiated and nurtured their faith. In contrast, the secessionists are urging the Christian to accept "new and advanced" doctrine.

love one another. This is a restatement of the second test (see also 2:9–11). Genuine Christians are those whose aim it is to live a life of love for others.

3:12–15 John begins his exposition of love with a negative illustration: Cain's murder of his brother Abel.

3:12 *belonged to the evil one.* Here John gives a specific example of what he meant in 3:8 when he said: "He who does what is sinful is of the devil." The killing of one's brother is the kind of evil that Satan inspires.

why did he murder him? John answers this question in the next sentence: "Because his own actions were evil and his brother's were righteous." Cain knew that in contrast to his brother's gift, his offering to God did not arise out of the desire to do right. Therefore, because of his anger, Cain slew his brother.

3:13 Cain is an example of how evil hates righteousness. John warns the believers that wicked people will hate them too when they do good. The conclusion that John draws from this story is that Christians must expect hostility from the world (see 3:1 and John 15:18–25; 17:14; 1 Peter 4:12–19).

3:14 *death.* Here "death" refers to the kingdom of

death—i.e., to the realm of Satan. In contrast, God's kingdom is characterized by life everlasting.

from death to life. The implication is that all people start out "dead." Satan is their father. They live in his realm. But by means of the rebirth process (which John mentioned in 2:29–3:2), it is possible to pass into the kingdom of life and become a child of God.

We know ... because we love. Love is evidence that one possesses eternal life.

3:15 Anyone who hates his brother is a murderer. Jesus makes this same link between hatred and murder (see Matt. 5:21–22). However, Jesus stopped short of saying what John does, namely that hatred is tantamount to murder.

3:16–17 John next offers a positive example of love: Jesus' sacrificial love for the human race. Both the example of Cain and the example of Jesus involve death. But Cain's act sprang from hatred and *took* the life of another while Jesus' act sprang from love and he *gave* his own life for others.

3:16 This is how we know what love is. John defines "love" not by means of an intellectual proposition, but by a practical example. Love is what Jesus demonstrated when he gave his life for others.

3:17 While only a few Christians will be called upon to make the supreme sacrifice of their lives for the sake of others, *all* Christians can and must constantly share their possessions in order to relieve the material suffering that abounds in this world.

brother. In verse 16 John used the plural "brothers." But here he becomes quite specific and asks his readers to consider the needs of a particular individual ("brother" is singular). "Loving everyone in general may be an excuse for loving nobody in particular" (Lewis).

pity. Such self-giving love is not without emotion, even though it is not primarily a feeling. John calls for genuine concern in the face of the plight of others.

3:18 But this "love" must be more than the mere verbal affirmation that, "Yes, I am committed to the idea of love." Genuine love shows itself in concrete deeds and in truth.

3:19–24 This section is a parenthesis in John's thought by which he both concludes the previous section and provides a bridge to the new unit. It is not easy, however, to follow John's thought-flow here as he links together the human and the divine

aspects of assurance. The important thing to notice is that he is talking about prayer.

3:19–20 John seems to be saying that Christians can be at peace with themselves even when their consciences trouble them. Such troubled consciences may be the result of introspection that has pointed out how feeble their attempts are to love others and how prone to sin they seem to be. But, as John points out, the basis of their confidence is the fact that it is God who will judge them and not their own hearts. They can trust themselves to his all-knowing justice because they have sought and found his forgiveness (see 1 Cor. 4:3–5).

3:19 truth. By this word John links this new section to the previous section. People can only "belong to the truth" (v. 19)—i.e., be a part of God's kingdom, when they act "in truth" (v. 18)—i.e., when they love genuinely.

3:20 he knows everything. The human conscience is not infallible, but God is. The implication is that God—who knows a person's innermost secrets—will be more merciful than the heart of that person which sees in part and understands in part.

3:22 Once again, John states a truth in a stark, unqualified way: if we ask, we will receive. Later, however, he will add the stipulation that people must ask "according to [God's] will" (5:14).

obey. Obedience is not the cause of answered prayer; it is the condition that motivates Christians to pray. Obedience is the evidence that they are moving in accordance with God's will, that they are in union with him, and that they will want to pray.

3:23–24 In these verses, John brings together the three issues which underlie the three tests by which believers can know they are truly children of God. He shows the interconnection between obedience (the moral test), love (the social test), and belief (the doctrinal test) and how these relate to the question of union with God.

3:24 Those who obey his commands live in him. Obedience and union are connected. God's command is to believe and love. Obedience to this command brings union with Christ. Looked at from the other way around, union brings the desire and the ability to obey. In other words, the outward, objective side of the Christian life (which is active love for others in obedience to the command of God) is connected to the inner, subjective experience of being in union with God.

39

UNIT 8—Test the Spirits / 1 John 4:1-6

Test the Spirits

4 *Dear friends, do not believe every spirit, but test the spirits to see whether they are from God, because many false prophets have gone out into the world. ²This is how you can recognize the Spirit of God: Every spirit that acknowledges that Jesus Christ has come in the flesh is from God, ³but every spirit that does not acknowledge Jesus is not from God. This is the spirit of the antichrist, which you have heard is coming and even now is already in the world.*

*⁴You, dear children, are from God and have overcome them, because the one who is in you is greater than the one who is in the world. ⁵They are from the world and therefore speak from the viewpoint of the world, and the world listens to them. ⁶We are from God, and whoever knows God listens to us; but whoever is not from God does not listen to us. This is how we recognize the Spirit*ᵃ *of truth and the spirit of falsehood.*

ᵃ6 Or *spirit*

READ
First Reading / First Impressions: John reminds me here of a:
- ❏ teacher prepping students for the final
- ❏ leader rebuking those who are not going along with his program
- ❏ pastor encouraging the congregation that they are going to make it in spite of troubles

Second Reading / Big Idea: Reading between the lines, what is going on that might prompt John to write this passage?

SEARCH
1. In your own words, what is the problem that John is addressing in this passage (v. 1; see notes)?

2. From 2:15,19,22; 3:13,23–24; 4:2 and 4:6, how do people motivated by God's Spirit differ from those motivated by other spirits in their attitudes toward:

   Christ?

   Christians?

   the world?

3. What hope does verse 4 provide for Christians as we face the pressures of dealing with falsehood (see notes)?

4. Who are the three pronouns in verses 4–6 referring to?

"you" (v. 4):

"they / them" (v. 5):

"we / us" (v. 6):

APPLY

Topical study concentrates on one word or subject and gleans everything from the passage about this topic. In this case, focus on the topic of cults. Study 2:18–27 (Unit 5) and this passage, writing out what characterizes (a) their origin (b) their teaching (c) their relationship to others and (d) the Christian's resources against them. First jot down the verse reference and the main idea it deals with. Then consider how what you found applies to one group today that proclaims "new" insights traditional Christians have "missed" (like the Jehovah's Witnesses or an Eastern religion offshoot).

VERSE	MAIN IDEA

APPLICATION TO ONE CONTEMPORARY GROUP

GROUP AGENDA

After the first part, read the Scripture out loud and divide into groups of 4. Then come back together for the third part.

TO BEGIN / 10–15 Min. (Choose 1 or 2)

1. How did you study for tests in school: Cram the night before? Pace yourself? Skim your notes? Blow it off?

2. What test can you remember causing you the most stress: A big test in school? A college entrance exam? A driver's test? An audition?

3. Growing up, when do you remember thinking, "I wish I had listened to what my parents said"?

TO GO DEEPER / 30 Min. (Choose 2 or 3)

1. If the false teachers denied that "Jesus Christ has come in the flesh," what have you learned from your study and the reference notes about what they were teaching about Jesus?

2. What do you believe about Jesus' nature? What difference does it make whether he was truly divine? Whether he was truly human?

3. Why do people from Christian backgrounds get involved with cults? What "power" equips you to overcome, or stand against, false prophets?

4. What guidelines here and elsewhere in 1 John would help you distinguish between legitimate differences of opinion and heresy?

5. CASE STUDY: A college freshman returns from her first year with an obviously heightened awareness of spirituality. She has had contact with Christian, Eastern and "New Age" groups and is attracted by the sincerity and depth of commitment she sees in each. However, she is bothered by how the Christians reject the others' teachings, whereas the others absorb Christian teaching into their own. What do you say when she asks you what you think about all this?

TO CLOSE / 15–30 Min.

1. Has your group assigned three people as a leadership core to start a new small group?

2. How did you answer the last part of APPLY?

3. How do you feel about opening up to this group? How has the group helped you work through some of your spiritual struggles and questions?

4. How would you like the group to pray for you?

42

NOTES

Summary. In the final verse of the previous unit, John describes how Christians can know that God lives in them. They know this because the Holy Spirit bears inner witness to this fact (3:24). But the problem is that the secessionists make this same claim! They say that God's Spirit speaks to them too. In fact, such private revelations are the source of their new doctrine. So, how can one distinguish between spirits? What is the difference between God's Spirit and false spirits? Is there an objective basis on which to accept or reject subjective claims? The answer relates to doctrine. That spirit which acknowledges that Jesus (the Messiah) came in the flesh is a spirit from God. Likewise, the opposite is true. Those spirits that do not acknowledge Jesus in this way are not from God (see also 2:20–23).

Thus in this unit John expands on the doctrinal test—the third way by which to distinguish between true and false Christianity. There are two parts to this test. The first question is: to what spirit does one listen? Unless that spirit acknowledges Jesus as the Messiah come in the flesh, it is not of God (v. 2). The second question is: are you in submission to apostolic doctrine? Unless individuals acknowledge the truth of the Gospel (as taught from the beginning by apostles such as John), they are not following "the Spirit of truth" (v. 6).

4:1 do not believe every spirit. Having just claimed that Christians know God lives in them because the Holy Spirit bears witness to this fact, John hastens on to qualify what he means. Not everything a spirit says is automatically of God. In fact, it is dangerous to accept uncritically everything that is said "in the name of God." Not everyone claiming inner revelation is hearing God's voice!

test. The test that John suggests by which to distinguish between spirits is doctrinal in nature. It has to do with who Jesus is. False spirits will not acknowledge that Jesus of Nazareth (a fully human man) is the incarnate Christ (the divine Son of God). Notice that the focus of this test is upon the *spirit* who is the source of the prophecy—not upon what is said. In other words, true prophecy is not distinguished from false prophecy by the content of the prophecy itself. The question is: is the source of this prophecy divine or diabolical? (See also 1 Cor. 12:1–3; 14:29; 1 Thessalonians 5:19–22.)

spirits. The issue is not whether supernatural spirits exist and actually inspire prophecy. This was assumed to be the case by almost everyone in the first century (see, for example, Mark 1:21–28, 32–34). The question Christians wrestled with was how to know what kind of spirit was speaking in any given situation. Are the secessionists telling the truth? Have they heard a fresh word from God? Did the Holy Spirit inspire this new doctrine? John provides them with a means whereby they can tell the difference between God's Spirit and false spirits.

from God. John uses this phrase in five of the six verses in this unit. By it, in verses 1–3, he seeks to indicate that certain spirits have their origin in God (as opposed to others that emanate from "the antichrist") and in verses 4 and 6 he points out that certain people are from God (as opposed to others who are "from the world").

prophets. Prophets are those men and women who claim to speak on God's behalf. They allow the Holy Spirit—or another spirit—to speak through them. John does not deny the reality or the value of prophecy. He simply warns against false prophets, much as Jesus did (see Matt. 7:15; Mark 13:22–23).

4:2 To deny that Jesus, the Messiah, was truly human is incompatible with divine inspiration. Prophets who will not affirm this confession of faith are not of God.

acknowledges. What John has in mind is not mere recognition of who Jesus is—since even the demons know him (Mark 1:24). Rather, what is called for is an open, positive, public declaration of faith in Jesus.

Jesus Christ has come in the flesh. This is the second of three places in this epistle in which John touches upon how the secessionists view the person of Jesus. In 2:22–23, John says that they deny that Jesus is the Christ (i.e., that he is the Messiah). (See note on 2:22.) Here he asserts that they deny that Jesus, the Messiah, came in the flesh. In 5:6 (the third and final place at which he deals with the question of Jesus' nature), John gets to the heart of the matter. What the secessionists are really denying is that Jesus—as the Messiah—could have died.

4:3 In verse 2 John focused on the positive: Those spirits who acknowledge Jesus are from God. Here he focuses on the negative: Those who do not acknowledge Jesus are not from God.

antichrist. John returns to a theme he first dealt with in 2:18–27 (see the notes on 2:18). In that section

John's concern was that believers not be led astray by those who are filled with the spirit of the antichrist. Here his concern is with the claims by his opponents that their new teachings are inspired by God.

4:4–6 John turns from his focus on prophets (true and false) to a consideration of those who follow each type of prophet. In verse 4 he directs his word to "you" (the Christians in Ephesus); in verse 5 he talks about "them" and "they" (the secessionists); while in verse 6 he talks about "we" (the apostles, of whom John is a representative).

4:4 *overcome.* The Christians to whom John writes have successfully resisted overtures by false prophets (the secessionists) to get them to believe new doctrines. They have not been deceived.

the one who is in you. It is not by means of their own unaided strength that they are able to resist these false prophets. The source of their power is the Spirit of God who resides in them.

the one who is in the world. Satan is the power at work in the world.

4:5 The false prophets, having been inspired by Satan, are readily heard and accepted by those who are likewise influenced by Satan.

4:6 In contrast to the "world" (which stands in opposition to God, God's truth, and God's people), there is the church (which both believes God's truth and seeks to live it out).

we / us. Since John shifts from "you" in verse 4 to "we" in verse 6 it would appear that here he has in mind not just Christians in general but, specifically, teachers of apostolic doctrine like himself. This is the only unambiguous criterion for truth that John offers: "We are from God and whoever knows God listens to us." Those who follow John and other teachers of apostolic doctrine are following the "Spirit of truth." While it is true the Spirit affirms what is truth for those who know God, the fact is that the secessionists also claim to be led by the Spirit. So this criterion for knowing who is really following God is, by itself, ambiguous. However, the secessionists do not follow John and on this basis are quite clearly outside the bounds of apostolic Christianity.

recognize. Those who respond positively to the apostolic preaching are those who are led by "the Spirit of truth"—a reference probably to the Holy Spirit.

UNIT 9—God's Love and Ours / 1 John 4:7-21

God's Love and Ours

⁷*Dear friends, let us love one another, for love comes from God. Everyone who loves has been born of God and knows God. ⁸Whoever does not love does not know God, because God is love. ⁹This is how God showed his love among us: He sent his one and only Son ᵃ into the world that we might live through him. ¹⁰This is love: not that we loved God, but that he loved us and sent his Son as an atoning sacrifice for ᵇ our sins. ¹¹Dear friends, since God so loved us, we also ought to love one another. ¹²No one has ever seen God; but if we love one another, God lives in us and his love is made complete in us.*

¹³*We know that we live in him and he in us, because he has given us of his Spirit. ¹⁴And we have seen and testify that the Father has sent his Son to be the Savior of the world. ¹⁵If anyone acknowledges that Jesus is the Son of God, God lives in him and he in God. ¹⁶And so we know and rely on the love God has for us.*

God is love. Whoever lives in love lives in God, and God in him. ¹⁷In this way, love is made complete among us so that we will have confidence on the day of judgment, because in this world we are like him. ¹⁸There is no fear in love. But perfect love drives out fear, because fear has to do with punishment. The one who fears is not made perfect in love.

¹⁹*We love because he first loved us. ²⁰If anyone says, "I love God," yet hates his brother, he is a liar. For anyone who does not love his brother, whom he has seen, cannot love God, whom he has not seen. ²¹And he has given us this command: Whoever loves God must also love his brother.*

ᵃ9 Or *his only begotten Son*   ᵇ10 Or *as the one who would turn aside his wrath, taking away*

READ

First Reading / First Impressions: What are two or three key words or phrases that you see here?

❑ _____   ❑ _____   ❑ _____

Second Reading / Big Idea: In your own words, write what you think is the key verse or point here.

SEARCH

1. "Love" is mentioned 27 times in this section. What can you learn here about love's:

origin (7a)?

connection with knowing God (7b–8,16)?

relationship to God's actions (9–10)?

effects in our lives (11,19–20)?

being made complete (12,17)?

relationship to fear (17–18)?

2. What do verses 8–15 teach about God? About Christ? About the Holy Spirit?

God, the Father	Jesus Christ	Holy Spirit

3. Read the story about John as an old man in the "Style" section of the Introduction on page 9. How do you react to John's reply that loving one another "is enough"? How does that statement fit with other assertions John makes in this epistle?

APPLY
Here is a chance to practice a little bit of what this passage is all about. Jot down the names of the people in your group in the left column. Then, in the right column, beside each name, jot down an affirmation for each person—that which you appreciate most about this person, or the contribution this person has made to your life. For instance: "John—his encouragement to me; Mary—her warmth and compassion"; etc. Then, when you meet as a group, ask one person to sit in silence while the others share what they jotted down about this person. Then take the next person and repeat the process until you have covered everyone in your group.

NAME	AFFIRMATION

GROUP AGENDA

After the first part, read the Scripture out loud and divide into groups of 4. Then come back together for the third part.

TO BEGIN / 10–15 Min. (Choose 1 or 2)

1. What were you afraid of as a child?

2. When have you written or received a "love letter"?

3. What family event or experience stands out as an example of your family at their closest?

TO GO DEEPER / 30 Min. (Choose 2 or 3)

1. If you have completed the homework, what stood out to you from READ or SEARCH?

2. Is the love discussed in this passage an action or a feeling? What does this tell you about love?

3. Why is it a lie to say you love God when you do not show that you love your "brother"?

4. If you want to do a better job of loving others, how should you go about it? What is the only way to improve (see vv. 15–16)?

5. How does the message that God's love drives out fear (v. 18) fit with the teaching that God is light (1:5)? When has God's love cast out fear in your life?

6. CASE STUDY: Chuck has really tried, but he simply cannot get along with his 16-year-old son. Chuck is a task-oriented, success-minded driver. He is hard on himself. He is hard on his son. His son, by temperament, is just the opposite. His room is a disaster. His school work is never done on time, and he won't "go out and get a job." Chuck is at his wit's end. What can you offer in the way of advice?

TO CLOSE / 15–30 Min.

1. Affirm each other, following the directions in APPLY.

2. Where do you have the greatest trouble loving people—at church, at work, or at home?

3. How can the group pray for you?

NOTES

Summary. In 3:23 John stated, "This is his command: to believe in the name of his Son, Jesus Christ, and to love one another as he commanded us." In the previous unit (Unit 8), John expanded on the first part of this command—believing in Jesus. In this unit he expands on the second part of the command—loving other people. John uses the word "love" some 43 times in his epistle; 27 of those times are in this unit.

4:7 For the third time John returns to the theme of love. In his first discussion he reminded his readers that love is a command and that to love is to live in the light (2:7–11). In his second discussion he pointed out that Jesus is the model of how to love others and that loving others is evidence that a person belongs to the truth (3:11–20). In this discussion he points out the basis on which he has said all this about love. It is because God himself is love!

love one another. John will use this phrase three times in the next five verses (see vv. 7,11,12). Each time, however, he uses it in a slightly different way. Here he urges his readers to love others because love originates in God.

Everyone who loves. Since "love comes from God," all acts of love are reflections of God's nature.

4:8 *Whoever does not love does not know God.* To claim to be a Christian without living a life of love "is like claiming to be intimate with a foreigner whose language we cannot speak, or to have been born of parents whom we do not in any way resemble" (Stott). Love is the language of God and the mark of his parentage.

God is love. This is the second great assertion that John makes in this epistle about the nature of God. (His first assertion is that God is light.) In the first century both these statements about God would have been unexpected. At that time in history there was a deep suspicion that the gods were dark and mysterious and that they cared little about human beings.

4:9–10 John now underlines what he said previously, both in his Gospel (John 3:16) and in this epistle (1 John 3:16): true love expresses itself in self-sacrificial action undertaken for the benefit of another person without regard to personal cost.

4:10 Love is initiated by God. Love is his posture toward the human race, and this love is given substance by the incarnation of his Son. It is not the other way around. People do not reach out to God with warm feelings or acts of devotion and thereby trigger his love for them. God is the primal lover. It is his action that draws out their response. Love begins with God.

an atoning sacrifice for our sins. By this phrase John describes the saving work that Jesus did on behalf of the human race. The idea of atonement is tied up with the Old Testament concept of substitution and sacrifice. In the Old Testament, sin was dealt with when a person symbolically placed his sins on an animal that he had brought to the temple. This animal had to be perfect—without spot or blemish. It was then sacrificed in place of the sinful (imperfect) person. Such substitutionary sacrifices were a picture of the final sacrifice Jesus would one day make for all men and women.

4:11 ***love one another.*** This is the second time John uses this phrase. The basis for his exhortation this time is the demonstrated fact that "God so loved us." Jesus' sacrificial death on behalf of the human race assures people that God loves them, and thus releases in them the ability to love others. Because they are loved they can love.

4:12 ***No one has ever seen God.*** It is not possible for a human being to see God in a direct, unscreened way. Such an encounter is beyond human capability. John reiterates here (and elsewhere) the biblical teachings on this matter. (See John 1:18; 5:37; 6:46; as well as Exodus 33:19–23.) Perhaps John finds it necessary to say this because some of the secessionists claim to have seen God.

love one another. In the third use of this phrase, John states that although God cannot be seen directly, his life can be experienced by people as they love one another. Since God is love, they know him when they love.

4:13–16 In these verses John elaborates on the phrase in verse 12: "God lives in us."

4:14–16 Christians have the Holy Spirit (v. 13) because they acknowledge that Jesus is the Son of God (vv. 14–15) and because they dwell in his unconditional love (v. 16).

4:17–21 Having completed his comments on what the statement means that "God lives in us," John next elaborates on a second phrase from verse 12: "his love is made complete in us."

4:17 ***confidence.*** Just as believers will have confidence at the second coming of Christ (2:28) and as

they have confidence when they approach God in prayer (3:19–22), so too they will also have confidence on the Day of Judgment.

we are like him. Once again—as he did in 3:6 and 9—John speaks about a future reality as if it were even now fully realized. In fact, as he has already stated (3:2), believers will not "be like him" until the Second Coming.

4:18 ***no fear in love.*** The reason for the confidence believers will have on the Day of Judgment is that they know God to be their father in whose love they have trusted. People cannot love and fear at the same moment; i.e., it is impossible to approach God with a heart filled both with servile fear and with an overflowing sense of his love for them and their love for him. The love casts out the fear.

fear has to do with punishment. This is the root of the fear: they think God is going to punish them. They forget that they are his forgiven children.

4:19 The love believers exhibit is a response to the prior love of God for them. Love begets love.

4:20 Love for God is not merely warm, inner feelings. Love is not love unless it finds concrete expression via active caring for others. Furthermore, since it is far easier to love a visible person than to love the invisible God, to claim success in the harder task (loving God) while failing in the easier task (loving others) is an absurd and hopeless contradiction.

a liar. Three times in this letter John has pointed out lies. It is a lie to claim to follow God and yet live in darkness by not keeping his commands (1:6; 2:4). It is a lie to claim God as Father while denying Jesus his Son (2:22–23). And here he says that it is a lie to claim to love God while hating others. These three lies parallel the three tests of a true Christian. The three lies are the reverse side of the moral, doctrinal and relational tests. The true Christian does not live in an immoral fashion, does not deny Jesus, and does not hate others. Holiness, faith and love verify the claim to be a child of God.

4:21 If people truly love God they will keep his commands; and his command is to love others—as John reminds his readers one more time as he ends this lesson on love (see also 2:9–11; 3:10,23). To love God and to love others is a single inseparable ordinance.

UNIT 10—Faith in the Son of God / 1 John 5:1-12

5 Everyone who believes that Jesus is the Christ is born of God, and everyone who loves the father loves his child as well. ²This is how we know that we love the children of God: by loving God and carrying out his commands. ³This is love for God: to obey his commands. And his commands are not burdensome, ⁴for everyone born of God overcomes the world. This is the victory that has overcome the world, even our faith. ⁵Who is it that overcomes the world? Only he who believes that Jesus is the Son of God.

⁶This is the one who came by water and blood—Jesus Christ. He did not come by water only, but by water and blood. And it is the Spirit who testifies, because the Spirit is the truth. ⁷For there are three that testify: ⁸theª Spirit, the water and the blood: and the three are in agreement. ⁹We accept man's testimony, but God's testimony is greater because it is the testimony of God, which he has given about his Son. ¹⁰Anyone who believes in the Son of God has this testimony in his heart. Anyone who does not believe God has made him out to be a liar, because he has not believed the testimony God has given about his Son. ¹¹And this is the testimony: God has given us eternal life, and this life is in his Son. ¹²He who has the Son has life; he who does not have the Son of God does not have life.

ª7,8 Late manuscripts of the Vulgate *testify in heaven: the Father, the Word and the Holy Spirit, and these three are one. ⁸And there are three that testify on earth: the* (not found in any Greek manuscript before the sixteenth century)

READ

First Reading / First Impressions: John here reminds me of:

- ❏ a pastor wrapping up the sermon
- ❏ a politician endorsing a candidate for office
- ❏ a lawyer making a final appeal to the jury

Second Reading / Big Idea: What's the main point or topic?

SEARCH

1. From verses 4–5, what is God's part and our part in "overcoming the world" (see notes)?

2. From verses 1 and 5, plus 2:22–23; 3:23; 4:2,15, what truths about Jesus must Christians affirm? What is the significance of each?

3. According to the study notes, how has God given witness to Jesus by:

water (see also John 1:29–34)?

blood (see also John 12:23–33)?

the Spirit (see also John 14:26; 15:26)?

4. The words "testimony," "testify" or "testifies" appear eight times here. Who is testifying about what to whom?

APPLY

Read the note for 5:10 on "believes in." How much does your *believing* Jesus go beyond that to *believing in* Jesus? What is one way you feel the new life of Jesus is breaking into your experience?

1 John 5:11–12 is probably the best Scripture in the Bible on assurance of eternal life for a Christian. If you have not committed these verses to memory, this week would be a good time to do so. First, reflect on what these verses mean to you: How do you respond to the matter of fact statements about God giving us "life"—for now and eternity? Jot down your thoughts in the space below. Then, write out these verses on a 3 x 5 card and place this card on your dashboard or over the kitchen sink, where you can repeat the verses several times a day—until you have committed them to memory.

GROUP AGENDA

After the first part, read the Scripture out loud and divide into groups of 4. Then come back together for the third part.

TO BEGIN / 10–15 Min. (Choose 1 or 2)

1. When you were growing up, what chore did you have that was a real burden?

2. In sports, what was the greatest victory you ever saw? What was the most agonizing defeat?

3. What part of a worship service helps to strengthen your faith the most?

TO GO DEEPER / 30 Min. (Choose 2 or 3)

1. From what is said here, what do you think the false teachers were teaching about Jesus Christ?

2. How do the water, blood and Spirit confirm that life is found in Jesus? What else from READ and SEARCH stands out to you?

3. What were some of the evidences that led you to believe that life is found in Jesus? Where do you struggle in your faith now?

4. Being totally honest, how "burdensome" do you find obeying God's commands (v. 3)?

5. CASE STUDY: Debbie, a member of your small group, struggles with "assurance of salvation." No matter how much she prays about it and talks to other believers, she still fears that she really isn't truly a Christian. She accepts that others possess that assurance, and she so desperately wants to enjoy it herself. How could you use this passage (see also 5:13) to help Debbie?

TO CLOSE / 15–30 Min.

1. How are you doing on your group mission?

2. Share your answer to one of the exercises in APPLY.

3. How can the group pray for you this week?

NOTES

Summary. This is the final unit in the epistle. (The last few verses will be given over to concluding remarks rather than to extending John's argument.) John has one last statement to make before he concludes his book. It has to do with Jesus. The crucial issue in this whole matter of orthodoxy versus apostasy hinges on one's view of Jesus. If faith is rightly directed at the historic Jesus, then (by implication) correct lifestyle and loving relationships will flow from that commitment. But if not—if the Jesus who is honored is more a product of fancy than fact—then quite a different worldview will flourish (as the secessionists demonstrate). So John ends where he began—with his testimony to Jesus.

In this final unit, John returns to the themes he struck in his prologue. The parallels between his first and last unit are strong. For example, in the prologue John spoke about testifying, "The life appeared; we have seen it and testify to it ..." (1:2). "Testimony" is also a key theme in this concluding unit. In the prologue, John also spoke about eternal life: "... we proclaim to you the eternal life" (1:2). (The word "life" appeared there three times.) So too here in the final unit one finds the concept of eternal life. (The word "life" is used four times in 5:4–12.)

5:1–4a Here John ties together the three tests of faith. "The real link between the three tests is seen to be the new birth. Faith, love and obedience are the natural outgrowth which follows a birth from above" (Stott).

5:3 *burdensome.* Obedience to the thousands of often picayune rules and regulations promulgated by the scribes and Pharisees was indeed a heavy burden. But obedience to God does not exasperate the Christian, since God's laws are of quite a different character (e.g., they are life-giving), and the faith of Christians provides the power for obedience.

5:4 *has overcome the world.* To the world, God's commands are a burden (v. 3); but not to Christians who by virtue of the new birth live in a new sphere. But what is this "victory that has overcome the world"? John might have in mind the past victory of Jesus via his death and resurrection (see John 16:33). In this case, Christians would participate in that victory by continuing to win over the world through the power of Jesus. Or John may have in view the conversion of each believer, which would be the moment he or she entered into the conquering power of Jesus. In either case, it is Jesus who has won the victory and Christians who continue to participate in it.

our faith. This is the source of the overcoming power of the Christian—confidence and trust that Jesus is the Son of God (see 5:5). It is by means of faith in Jesus that Christians can win over the world which stands in opposition to them as they seek to follow the ways of God.

5:6–9 How is it that a person comes to faith in Jesus? By means of reliable witnesses, John answers. In these verses he names three such witnesses that testify to who Jesus is and what he has done. These three witnesses are the water, the blood and the Holy Spirit.

5:6 *by water and blood.* By these two phrases, John probably is referring to Jesus' baptism and Jesus' death. These two events are crucial in understanding who Jesus really is. The secessionists felt that Jesus, the man, became the Christ at his baptism and that the Christ then departed prior to the death of Jesus. In contrast, the apostolic witness (as recorded in the New Testament) asserts that at his baptism, Jesus publicly identified himself with the sins of the people (even though he himself was without sin). And at his death, Jesus died to take away those sins. Water and blood also function as symbols of purification and redemption. This was their meaning in the rituals described in Leviticus. Furthermore, they would also remind John's readers of the ordinances of baptism and communion. Some scholars feel that the "water and the blood" refer to the single event of Jesus' crucifixion during which "water and blood" flowed from his side.

Jesus Christ. So as to drive home his point, John uses this dual title which displays the inextricable unity of the divine and human in this one person. He is Jesus of Nazareth and he is the Messiah sent by God. It was Jesus Christ—and not just a human named Jesus—who experienced both baptism and death.

not ... *by water only.* The secessionists agree that the baptism of Jesus was all important. They felt it was then that the heavenly Christ infused the man Jesus. (In fact, it was the Holy Spirit who descended on Jesus at his baptism.) John is insistent that both the Baptism and the Crucifixion are crucial in understanding Jesus. If it was only a human named Jesus who died on the cross (as John's opponents thought), then universal forgiveness for sin would be impossible. But, in fact, it was Jesus, *the Messiah*, who died on the cross. Furthermore, it would be a lie that God sent his only Son to die for the world (as

John states in his Gospel in 3:16), if it had been only a human named Jesus who was crucified.

it is the Spirit who testifies. John has already stated that there is an inner witness given by the Holy Spirit as to the truth of who Jesus is (see 3:24 and 4:13 as well as 1 Cor. 12:3). In verses 6–11 John will use the verb "to testify, or bear witness" four times and the noun "testimony or witness" six times.

the Spirit is the truth. The Holy Spirit is the third witness, and is qualified to be such because the Spirit is, in his essence, truth itself.

5:7 *three that testify.* There are two kinds of testimony: the objective historical witness of the water and the blood (Jesus identified himself with the sins of the people at his baptism and then died for these sins on the cross); and the subjective, experiential witness of the Spirit (Christians experience within themselves the reality of these events). These two types of witness complement one another. Believers know in their hearts the truthfulness and power of the historical facts of Jesus' life and death.

5:9 John now clarifies the authority behind these three witnesses. It is God himself. In addition, the object of the three-fold witness is made explicit. It is Jesus his Son.

greater. In a law court, testimony is accepted when it is corroborated by two or three witnesses (see Deut. 19:15). How much more substantial is the three-fold testimony of God?

5:10–12 Here John points out the result of believing this triple testimony. The believer gains eternal life. The purpose of this testimony is to produce faith. To accept the testimony is synonymous with believing in Jesus.

5:10 *believes in.* It is one thing to *believe* Jesus. It is another to *believe in* Jesus. To believe Jesus is to accept what he says as true. To believe in Jesus is to accept who he is. It is to trust him completely and to commit one's life to him.

a liar. To reject this triple testimony is to disbelieve God (who is himself the essence of truth). It is to attribute falsehood to God (see 1:10).

5:11 *eternal life.* In receiving the testimony and thus receiving the Son, one also receives eternal life. The Greek word which is here translated "eternal" means "that which belongs to the coming age." But since that age has already broken into the present age, eternal life can be enjoyed even now.

UNIT 11—Concluding Remarks / 1 John 5:13-21

Concluding Remarks

¹³*I write these things to you who believe in the name of the Son of God so that you may know that you have eternal life.* ¹⁴*This is the confidence we have in approaching God: that if we ask anything according to his will, he hears us.* ¹⁵*And if we know that he hears us—whatever we ask—we know that we have what we asked of him.*

¹⁶*If anyone sees his brother commit a sin that does not lead to death, he should pray and God will give him life. I refer to those whose sin does not lead to death. There is a sin that leads to death. I am not saying that he should pray about* that. ¹⁷*All wrongdoing is sin, and there is sin that does not lead to death.*

¹⁸*We know that anyone born of God does not continue to sin; the one who was born of God keeps him safe, and the evil one cannot harm him.* ¹⁹*We know that we are children of God, and that the whole world is under the control of the evil one.* ²⁰*We know also that the Son of God has come and has given us understanding, so that we may know him who is true. And we are in him who is true—even in his Son Jesus Christ. He is the true God and eternal life.*

²¹*Dear children, keep yourselves from idols.*

READ

First Reading / First Impressions: If you were part of the church John was writing to, what feeling would you have as you finished reading or hearing his letter?

Second Reading / Big Idea: In this conclusion, what verse is most important to you? Why?

SEARCH

1. Compare verse 13 with John 20:31. What do these reveal about what is really important to John?

2. How does the awareness that we have God's kind of life affect our prayer life (v. 14; see note)?

3. What does John mean by the condition to this promise (v. 14; see note)?

4. What is the significance of the promise in verse 15 to you (see notes)?

52

5. In light of Mark 3:22–30 and the false teachers that are plaguing this church, what type of person might John mean by verse 16b (see notes)?

6. How is the life of the Christian related to the life of Christ in the promises of verse 18?

APPLY

What "idol" of the world tempts you away from steadily following Christ today? What can you do practically to "keep yourself" from that idol?

What is one major thing you want to work on as a result of studying this letter?

Here's a chance to take God up on his invitation to come to him with your concerns. Take a moment and jot down in the left column three or four things that are concerns to you right now. For instance: "my family ... my finances ... my future work." Then, in the right column, for each concern jot down one specific thing you want to ask of God. For instance: "my family—more closeness and better communication," etc. When you have finished making your "prayer list," spend some time with God talking about these concerns. Then, when you get together with your group, you may want to spend some more time praying together about these concerns.

MY CONCERNS	MY PRAYER REQUESTS

"This is the confidence we have in approaching God: that if we ask anything according to his will, he hears us. And if we know that he hears us—whatever we ask—we know that we have what we asked of him."—1 John 5:14–15

GROUP AGENDA

After the first part, read the Scripture out loud and divide into groups of 4. Then come back together for the third part.

TO BEGIN / 10–15 Min. (Choose 1 or 2)

1. Did you say a bedtime prayer as a child? What kind of prayer? Did your parents join you?

2. What came closest to being the "unpardonable sin" in your family when you were growing up?

3. Who was your "idol" as a kid?

TO GO DEEPER / 30 Min. (Choose 2 or 3)

1. What does it mean to pray according to God's will?

2. Based on your study and the reference notes, what is the "sin that leads to death"? Why do the very fears of those who worry about having committed this sin prove that they have not done so?

3. Was there anything else from this passage or from READ or SEARCH that you would like to discuss or share?

4. When, if ever, have you doubted whether your faith in God was real? With how much confidence can you say now that you "know that you have eternal life" (v. 13)?

5. With how much confidence do you "approach God" (v. 14) in prayer? What do you do when you feel like your prayers are just "bouncing off the ceiling"?

6. CASE STUDY: Two of your closest friends are not professing Christians. One says that she was a Christian once, but now she would "rather have fun." The other openly ridicules the Christian faith as a "bunch of myths." How should you pray for these friends?

TO CLOSE / 15–30 Min.

1. How did your group answer the three "Brainstorming" questions on page M19 in the center section)?

2. What did you write for one of the first two questions in APPLY?

3. If you feel comfortable doing so, share the prayer concerns you listed in APPLY.

4. How can the group join you in prayer?

NOTES

Summary. John concludes his epistle with some final comments which relate to the needs of his congregation. Now that his argument against the secessionists is over, John's style changes. He begins to speak more like a pastor than a polemicist. He now speaks directly to the needs of the congregations in Ephesus. In particular, he is anxious that they be encouraged. His encouragement comes in the form of a series of assurances. He begins by assuring them that they do have eternal life since they "believe in the name of the Son of God" (v. 13). He then assures them that God hears and answers prayer (vv. 14–17). Finally, writing in almost a poetic fashion, he assures them that they will be kept safe from a life of habitual sin (v. 18); that they are indeed children of God (v. 19); and that they do, indeed, know the truth (v. 20).

5:13–17 The previous unit ended with John pointing out that to possess the Son was to possess life and that those who do not possess the Son do not possess life. Just as he has done several times already in this letter when he has described both the positive and the negative side of an issue, he then hastens to reassure his readers that they are on the right side and so in no danger. In these verses he assures them that since they believe "in the name of the Son of God" they do, indeed, have eternal life.

5:13 This verse parallels John 20:31, which is the concluding verse of the Gospel. (John 21 is an epilogue.) In his Gospel John writes: "But these are written that you may believe that Jesus is the Christ, the Son of God, and that by believing you may have life in his name." John wrote his Gospel in order to witness to Jesus and so inspire faith in those who did not yet know Christ. By believing in Jesus, they would discover "life." His purpose in the epistle is similar, except that now his words are directed to those who have, in fact, come to believe in Jesus. His purpose is no longer to tell them how to find "life" but, instead, to assure them that they do have eternal life—no matter what the secessionists might say.

eternal life. The primary meaning of this phrase is not "that which lasts forever" (though this is implied). Rather, what is in view is the very life of God himself which is shared with Christians through Jesus Christ.

5:14–17 Not only do Christians enjoy the assurance of eternal life, they have a second assurance: that God will answer their prayers.

5:14 confidence. Originally this word meant "freedom of speech." It was used to describe the right of all those in a democracy to speak their mind. By this word John refers to the bold confidence Christians have—that they can approach God in prayer and freely speak their minds.

according to his will. In 3:22, John says that the condition for answered prayer is obedient behavior: we "receive from him [God] anything we ask, because we obey his commands and do what pleases him." Here John adds another condition: what we ask must be in accord with God's purposes (see also Matt. 26:39,42). "Prayer rightly considered is not a device for employing the resources of omnipotence to fulfill our own desires, but a means by which our desires may be redirected according to the mind of God, and made into channels for the forces of his will" (C.H. Dodd).

5:15 he hears us. By this phrase John means "he hears us favorably." To know that God hears is to know that "we have what we asked."

we have what we asked. "Our petitions are granted at once: the results of the granting are perceived in the future" (Plummer).

5:16 John now offers an illustration of how prayer operates. He is probably not using the term "brother" to refer to other Christians, but rather in the broader sense of "neighbors" or possibly even as "nominal church members." This is evident from how he writes about these people. He says that Christians ought to pray that God will give "life" to a "brother" whose sin "does not lead to death." This is not the prayer one prays for Christians who already have eternal life as John has just pointed out in verses 11–12. (This broader use of the word "brother" is also found in 3:16–17 as well as in Matt. 5:22–24 and 7:3–5.)

a sin that leads to death. Although John's readers probably understood what he was referring to, it is not at all clear to the modern reader just what this phrase means. A specific kind of sin is probably not in view here but rather a lifestyle of habitual, willing and persistent sinning. Perhaps what John has in mind are people like some of the Pharisees he and the other apostles encountered when they were with Jesus. These men saw Jesus' works and heard his words and yet still pronounced that he was empowered by Satan (Mark 3:22–30). To call good, evil, to understand light to be darkness, is evidence of a mindset that would never call upon God for forgiveness. And if one does not ask, forgiveness cannot be granted. And so one goes to death unrepentant and unforgiven.

I am not saying that he should pray about that. While John does not forbid prayer for those involved in a "sin that leads to death," he does not advise it since he doubts its value in such a case.

5:18 John concludes with a final list of assurances, written in almost poetic style. The first affirmation relates to Christian behavior: "It expresses the truth, not that he [the Christian] cannot ever slip into acts of sin, but rather that he does not persist in it habitually. ... The new birth results in new behaviour. Sin and the child of God are incompatible. They may occasionally meet; they cannot live together in harmony" (Stott).

the one who was born of God. By this phrase John refers to Jesus Christ. In the past he has referred to Christians in a similar way (2:29; 3:9; 4:7; 5:1,4). In other words, almost identical phrases are used to describe both the Christian and the Christ.

5:19 The second affirmation which John makes is that they are, indeed, "children of God." They are part of the family of God and in relationship with the other children of God. This assertion comes in the form of a categorical statement: either a person is "of God" or a person is of "the world" and, as John has already shown, the world is under the control of Satan. John offers no third category. He assures those who are "born of God" (v. 18) that they are "children of God."

5:20 The third affirmation is that they really do know what is true (over against the secessionists who are promoting a new truth). John asserts this fact in several ways. First, the source of their insight is "the Son of God" who "has given us understanding." The purpose of this understanding is so that they can know "him who is true." Second, it is not just that in knowing Christ they accept his teachings to be true. It is deeper than that. They are "in him who is true." Truth is not something external. They are "in" the truth and the truth is "in them." Furthermore, to be in the Son is to be in the "true God" and share his very life.

5:21 idols. Whether John has specific idols in mind is not clear. He may mean: "Do not abandon the real for the illusory" (Blaiklock). His imperative may refer either to the false images of the heretical teachers which created a form of idolatry or it may refer to the pagan idols that filled the city of Ephesus. Ephesus was the site of the great temple of Diana which was one of the wonders of the ancient world. It was also the site of immoral rites and the haunt of criminals (because they could not be arrested while in the temple). Its influence permeated the city.

UNIT 12—No Hospitality for False Prophets / 2 John

¹The elder,

To the chosen lady and her children, whom I love in the truth—and not I only, but also all who know the truth—²because of the truth, which lives in us and will be with us forever:

³Grace, mercy and peace from God the Father and from Jesus Christ, the Father's Son, will be with us in truth and love.

⁴It has given me great joy to find some of your children walking in the truth, just as the Father commanded us. ⁵And now, dear lady, I am not writing you a new command but one we have had from the beginning. I ask that we love one another. ⁶And this is love: that we walk in obedience to his commands. As you have heard from the beginning, his command is that you walk in love.

⁷Many deceivers, who do not acknowledge Jesus Christ as coming in the flesh, have gone out into the world. Any such person is the deceiver and the antichrist. ⁸Watch out that you do not lose what you have worked for, but that you may be rewarded fully. ⁹Anyone who runs ahead and does not continue in the teaching of Christ does not have God; whoever continues in the teaching has both the Father and the Son. ¹⁰If anyone comes to you and does not bring this teaching, do not take him into your house or welcome him. ¹¹Anyone who welcomes him shares in his wicked work.

¹²I have much to write to you, but I do not want to use paper and ink. Instead, I hope to visit you and talk with you face to face, so that our joy may be complete.

¹³The children of your chosen sister send their greetings.

READ
First Reading / First Impressions: If I received this letter, I would feel:
- ❏ greatly encouraged
- ❏ like I had contributed to a problem John had to straighten out
- ❏ like John must have been in a hurry to get this letter out

Second Reading / Big Idea: What's the main point or topic?

SEARCH
1. What connections do you find between John's themes of "truth," "love" and "obedience" in verses 1–6?

2. How have the "deceivers" (v. 7) lost sight of this connection?

3. In "running ahead" of the apostles' teaching, what would a person leave behind (vv. 8–9; see notes)?

4. What potential problems might occur if the church was to offer support and hospitality to these traveling teachers (vv. 10–11; see notes)?

APPLY

When it comes to balancing truth and love, which side do you tend to emphasize more? Why?

What guidelines do you use to decide what missionaries or organizations to support?

This would be a good chance to check up on your hospitality motives. Think of the people you have invited to your home or taken out for a meal in the last six months. Jot down their names or initials in the left column. Then, in the right column, jot down who the person is and why you invited this person. For instance: John and Susan Smith—old college friends—strictly social; Brenda Ackers—business associate—felt she was lonely after her divorce; etc. If you have time, go over the list and code each person with the following symbols in the margin:
- TBH = To be helpful to someone who is hurting, lonely or in need
- JFF = Just for fun and a good time
- DCF = Deep Christian fellowship around Jesus Christ

Analyze your coding to discover what motivates you in offering hospitality.

MY DINNER GUESTS	WHO THEY ARE AND WHY I INVITED THEM

GROUP AGENDA

After the first part, read the Scripture out loud and divide into groups of 4. Then come back together for the third part.

TO BEGIN / 10–15 Min. (Choose 1 or 2)

1. When you were growing up, where did you gather for family reunions? What was special about these times?

2. How often did you have guests stay in your home? Where did you put them up?

3. Whose home do you remember for their warm Christian hospitality?

TO GO DEEPER / 30 Min. (Choose 2 or 3)

1. What do you think was the situation that caused John to write this letter?

2. Why is John so dogmatic about believers not opening their homes to false teachers?

3. How do we "open our homes" to false teachers today?

4. Have you ever had to terminate a relationship over some issue related to your faith? What was the issue? Would you still do so today?

5. Since there are so many charlatans in religious clothing, how do you overcome the tendency to just ignore all appeals for money?

6. CASE STUDY: Your friends Peter and Jane are a generous Christian couple who believe, on the basis of Luke 6:30, that they should give to "whomever the Lord leads to ask us for help since all we have comes from him, and he brings to us those whom we can help." What do you think?

TO CLOSE / 15–30 Min.

1. Are you planning a kickoff for starting a new small group? Have you made plans for celebrating your time together as a group?

2. What was your response to one of the first two questions in APPLY?

3. What did you discover in the last part of APPLY? (You don't need to share any specific names.)

4. How can the group pray for you?

NOTES

Summary. Second and Third John are the shortest letters in the New Testament; so short in fact that virtually everyone concedes that they are genuine. Who would bother to fake such brief, unassuming documents? Their length, incidentally, was determined by the size of a standard sheet (8 x 10 inches). Each letter fits exactly on one sheet.

There is a great similarity in both style and content between 2 and 3 John. (For example, compare 2 John 1 and 3 John 1; 2 John 4 and 3 John 4; 2 John 12 and 3 John 13–14.) Undoubtedly, both letters were written by the same person. There is also a close connection between 1 John and these two shorter letters (e.g., compare 1 John 4:3 and 2 John 7). All three epistles deal with the same general issues. Therefore, it is highly likely that the "elder" who identifies himself as the author of 2 and 3 John is, indeed, the apostle John who wrote 1 John.

The issue that motivated the writing of 2 and 3 John is that of wandering missionaries. In the days before modern motels (in a time when Roman inns were notorious for being dirty and flea-infested), visiting Christian teachers would turn to the local church for hospitality. The problem was that some of the people seeking room and board were false teachers espousing erroneous doctrines, while others were phonies, pretending to be true prophets but actually only concerned about free hospitality. Even the pagan Greek author Lucian was aware of this kind of abuse of hospitality. In his satirical work *Peregrinus*, he writes about a religious charlatan who lived off the generosity of the church as a way to avoid working. In an attempt to cope with this problem, an early church document called the *Didache* laid down a series of regulations guiding the reception of itinerant ministers. It said, for example, that true prophets were indeed to be entertained—for a day or two. But if a prophet stayed three days this was a sign that he was false. Likewise, if a prophet under the inspiration of the Spirit asked for money, this showed that he was a false prophet.

These are the concerns dealt with in 2 and 3 John. In 2 John, the author discusses false prophets. "Do not welcome such," he says. But in 3 John, he addresses the opposite problem: the failure of Christians to provide hospitality for genuine teachers.

vv. 1–3 As was the custom in first-century letters, the writer of this epistle first identifies himself, then he names the recipients of the letter, and concludes his salutation by pronouncing a blessing.

v. 1 *The elder.* This title appears to be used here in its natural sense (the author is elderly) rather than in its official sense (to designate a leader of the church). John is the last surviving apostle. He is now in his waning years. He is "*the* elder," not "*an* elder." It is not necessary to give his proper name. Everyone knows who he is.

the chosen lady. It is not clear whether John is addressing an actual person or a church which he personifies by this title. Probably he was referring to a church.

vv. 4–11 This is the heart of John's message. In verses 4–6 he focuses on the internal life of the local church. He points out its need to walk in truth, obedience and love. In verses 7–11 he focuses on the external life of the local church, specifically the threat to it posed by false teachers who espouse erroneous doctrine. John makes a sharp distinction between what is true (vv. 4–6) and what is false (vv. 7–11); between Christ and "the antichrist"; and between the commands of God and the deceptions of Satan.

v. 4 *commanded us.* Truth is not an option for the Christian. To depart from truth is to disobey God.

vv. 5–6 Not only are Christians commanded to believe and obey ("walk in the truth"), they are commanded to love one another. Love is expressed in obedience and obedience is shown in love.

vv. 7–11 John now turns from true believers to false deceivers. He warns Christians not to be deceived (vv. 7–8). He tells them not to encourage false teachers by giving them hospitality (vv. 10–11). If his exhortations in verses 4–6 to walk in truth, love and obedience are followed, the believers will be able to resist the heresy being taught by these false teachers.

v. 7 John first defines their error. They have a faulty view of Jesus. They deny the Incarnation.

have gone out. John may be saying that these false teachers were once members of the church but have now left (see 1 John 2:19). Or he may be saying that in the same way that the emissaries of God are sent out into the world (John 17:18; 20:21), Satan sends out his own emissaries.

the deceiver and the antichrist. These false teachers both deceive people and oppose Christ. Jesus also warned his followers about false prophets (Mark 13:5–6,22).

v. 8 *Watch out.* Having stated the problem, John then issues his first warning: do not cease in your vigilance.

do not lose. Failure to be vigilant could result in the loss of reward.

be rewarded fully. The Greek word translated "rewarded" refers to "the wages of a workman." John's concern is not with the loss of salvation which one does not earn in any case (it is a free gift), but with the loss of due reward for faithful service. However, if people are vigilant, they will gain the wages they have earned.

v. 9 *runs ahead.* The Greek word means "to go out in advance." It is used sarcastically here. It is likely that the false teachers were encouraging people to follow their "advanced" views which were based on their "special and superior" insights, in contrast to the "primitive" views of the apostles. John warns his readers that to leave basic Christianity is to run ahead of God.

does not have God. The false teachers were claiming that they knew God apart from the teachings of Christ. John asserts that this is not possible (see John 1:18; 14:6–9; 1 John 5:20).

v. 10 John now issues his second warning: do not receive or welcome false teachers into your home. This injunction sounds harsh in the light of the New Testament's insistence upon hospitality—including John's own words on the subject (see Rom. 12:13; 1 Tim. 3:2; Titus 1:8; Heb. 13:2; 1 Peter 4:8–10; 3 John 5–8). However, it is important to notice that John refers to teachers. This injunction is not directed at believers who might hold errant views. These false teachers were dangerous because they were like merchants trying to sell a new product (they "bring" into the house the wrong "teaching"). However, John may only be referring here to an "official welcome" by the church and he may mean to deny this only to teachers who deny the Incarnation (v. 7).

v. 11 Now he gives his reason for the warning: to welcome such a person would encourage an evil work that cuts people off from the Father by denying the Son.

v. 12 *much to write.* The elder has much more to say but he limits himself to one sheet of papyrus, preferring to speak to them in person. In Greek the idiom "face to face" is literally "mouth to mouth."

v. 13 The members of the church from which John writes send greetings.

UNIT 13—Be Hospitable to Genuine Teachers / 3 John

¹The elder,

To my dear friend Gaius, whom I love in the truth.

²Dear friend, I pray that you may enjoy good health and that all may go well with you, even as your soul is getting along well. ³It gave me great joy to have some brothers come and tell about your faithfulness to the truth and how you continue to walk in the truth. ⁴I have no greater joy than to hear that my children are walking in the truth.

⁵Dear friend, you are faithful in what you are doing for the brothers, even though they are strangers to you. ⁶They have told the church about your love. You will do well to send them on their way in a manner worthy of God. ⁷It was for the sake of the Name that they went out, receiving no help from the pagans. ⁸We ought therefore to show hospitality to such men so that we may work together for the truth.

⁹I wrote to the church, but Diotrephes, who loves to be first, will have nothing to do with us. ¹⁰So if I come, I will call attention to what he is doing, gossiping maliciously about us. Not satisfied with that, he refuses to welcome the brothers. He also stops those who want to do so and puts them out of the church.

¹¹Dear friend, do not imitate what is evil but what is good. Anyone who does what is good is from God. Anyone who does what is evil has not seen God. ¹²Demetrius is well spoken of by everyone—and even by the truth itself. We also speak well of him, and you know that our testimony is true.

¹³I have much to write you, but I do not want to do so with pen and ink. ¹⁴I hope to see you soon, and we will talk face to face.

Peace to you. The friends here send their greetings. Greet the friends there by name.

READ

First Reading / First Impressions: The real intent of this letter seems to be:
- ❏ a commendation of Gaius
- ❏ a condemnation of Diotrephes
- ❏ a recommendation for Demetrius

Second Reading / Big Idea: What do you see as the key sentence in this letter?

SEARCH

1. What conflicts were going on that prompted John to write this letter?

2. In what way does this letter tackle the hospitality issue differently than 2 John (see note on vv. 5–8)?

3. Why would it be so important that these traveling teachers be provided for by the local churches (vv. 6–8; see notes)?

4. From the information here and your "sanctified imagination," write a short character sketch of:

Gaius

Diotrephes

Demetrius

5. Specifically, how does Gaius' "love" (v. 6) differ from Diotrephe's "love" (v. 9)?

APPLY

What are some practical ways you can reflect Gaius' desire to help itinerant Christian workers today?

What is one thing you want to change in your life so you might be spoken of as John spoke of Gaius and Demetrius (and not of Diotrephes)?

This being the last session in this course, this would be a good time to stop and take inventory. On the lines below, put two marks to indicate where you are—somewhere between the two extremes:

x = where I was at the beginning of this course or group
o = where I am right now

ON KNOWING THE CORE OF WHAT I BELIEVE
Completely in the dark_____The lights have turned on

ON KNOWING WHERE I STAND ON ISSUES AND WHY
Completely in the dark_____The lights have turned on

ON KNOWING WHAT GOD WANTS ME TO DO WITH MY LIFE
Completely in the dark_____The lights have turned on

ON KNOWING WHAT GOD WANTS ME TO DO IN MY CHURCH AND COMMUNITY
Completely in the dark_____The lights have turned on

GROUP AGENDA

After the first part, read the Scripture out loud and divide into groups of 4. Then come back together for the third part.

TO BEGIN / 10–15 Min. (Choose 1 or 2)

1. Did you ever run out of money when you were away from home? What did you do?

2. Who extended loving hospitality to you when you needed it most?

3. Do you find opening up to new people easy or difficult?

TO GO DEEPER / 30 Min. (Choose 2 or 3)

1. Quickly go through the questions in SEARCH. (Those who have done the homework could take turns answering the questions.)

2. How did you answer the first two questions in APPLY?

3. What tensions in this early church do you see reflected in some way in churches today?

4. Has suspicion about the false motives or messages of some pastors or teachers soured you against them all? What needs to change so you won't hinder the work of God by failing to encourage his true servants?

5. CASE STUDY: A friend tells you that an elder in your church told him he should not support missionaries who aren't connected with the denomination, since they are not accountable to the church. Your friend, however, was brought to faith by one of these organizations. What would be your advice in light of 3 John?

TO CLOSE / 15–30 Min.

1. Share your responses to the last part of APPLY.

2. What have you gained the most from this course? What did you appreciate most about the group?

3. Have you finalized your plans for the future of your group?

4. How can this group remember you in prayer?

NOTES

Summary. In another short letter, this time addressed to a dear friend, John touches upon the question of itinerant teachers one more time. This time the problem is not with false teachers. The teachers in this letter are true Christians, working "for the sake of the Name" and therefore worthy to receive hospitality. John commends his friend Gaius for opening his home to them even though they were strangers to him. This is the flip side of the issue that was dealt with in 2 John. There John made it quite clear that the church must not give hospitality to false teachers. But here he says that it should and must welcome genuine teachers into its midst.

v. 1 *The elder.* Both 2 and 3 John were written by the same person, identified only as "the elder." The elder, as it has been argued, is none other than the apostle John. See the note on 2 John 1.

To my dear friend. This is one of only two personal letters in the New Testament. (The other is Philemon.) While certain other letters do bear the name of an individual recipient—for example, Timothy and Titus—they are, in fact, letters meant to be read publicly.

Gaius. There are several men by this name mentioned in the New Testament (see Acts 19:29; 20:4; Rom. 16:23; 1 Cor. 1:14). However, "Gaius" was one of the most common names in the Roman Empire. As a result it is not possible to identify with certainty the Gaius to whom John writes with any other Gaius in the New Testament. What is clear about this particular Gaius is that John had a high and affectionate regard for him; that he freely offered Christian hospitality to others; and that he was a leader in the local church.

whom I love in the truth. Truth is the sphere in which love flourishes (see 2 John 1–6).

v. 2 It was not uncommon for Greek letters to begin with a wish that the recipient would enjoy good health.

all may go well. The single Greek word which is translated by this phrase means, literally, "have a good journey." It eventually came to mean "prosper" or "succeed."

even as your soul is getting along well. This is, literally, "as your soul prospers." John desires spiritual as well as physical well-being for his friend.

v. 3 John knows that Gaius' "soul" is "getting along well" (as he says in v. 2) because of the news he received about him from "some brothers" who had visited him.

faithfulness to the truth. This was one of several characteristics of Gaius that John singles out for commendation. As John said over and over again in his first epistle, it is important that Christians adhere to the truth of the Gospel. Gaius had done just this. In verse 6, John will point out a second characteristic of Gaius: he loved others. This is another trait that is characteristic of the true Christian as defined by John in his first epistle. Gaius' life was a living demonstration of the "truth in love" that John speaks of in 1 John 3:18 and 2 John 1–6.

v. 4 *my children.* Paul used this phrase to describe those whose conversion to Christ he assisted. Perhaps, therefore, Gaius is John's spiritual son.

walking in the truth. Gaius did not just know the truth, he did it. He lived what he believed. He let his theological convictions guide his moral behavior.

vv. 5–8 Here John commends Gaius for showing hospitality to the visiting teachers. John's words in verses 5–8 stand in sharp contrast to what he wrote in 2 John 10–11 where he warned against offering hospitality to certain teachers. The difference is that in 2 John he was concerned about false teachers and here he discusses "brothers" who went out "for the sake of the Name" and who "work ... for the truth." Second and Third John must be read together to get a balanced picture of the situation in the early church when it came to itinerant teachers.

vv. 5–6 Having commended Gaius for "walking in the truth," John now points to a concrete example of what this actually involves. Gaius opened his house to some fellow Christians even though he did not know them. This is love in action. These visiting Christian teachers, at some later date, spoke appreciatively to John about the hospitality Gaius showed them.

v. 5 *strangers.* What pleases John especially is that Gaius opened his home to those he did not know personally.

v. 6 *send them on their way in a manner worthy of God.* Not only did he host these visitors while they were in town, but he provided them with provisions (probably food and money) to be used on the next leg of the journey. The verb used here, which means literally "to send forward," came to refer in this context to providing missionaries with supplies

for their onward journey (see Acts 15:3; Rom. 15:24; 1 Cor. 16:6,11; 2 Cor. 1:16; Titus 3:13).

v. 7 *the Name.* Jesus Christ.

they went out. This term was used to describe setting out on a mission for Christ. In other words, these visitors were not ordinary travelers, but Christian missionaries.

receiving no help from the pagans. John is not saying that they could not accept gifts from pagans, but that as a matter of policy they did not do so—unlike many of the itinerant non-Christian teachers of that era. "Devotees of various religions tramped the roads, extolling the virtues of the deity of their choice and collecting subscriptions from the public" (C.H. Dodd).

v. 8 "If the first reason for entertaining traveling missionaries is that they are brethren whom we should honor for setting out for the sake of the Name, the second is the much more practical one that they have no other means of support" (Stott).

hospitality. The ancient world saw hospitality as almost a sacred duty. For example, there was in operation at that time a system of "guest friendships" whereby families agreed to look after each other's members as they traveled through their community. Such hospitality was claimed by presenting a "token" that identified the traveler.

vv. 9–10 John sets in contrast to the hospitality of Gaius the hostility of Diotrephes.

v. 9 *Diotrephes.* He and Gaius may have been members of the same congregation or, more likely, of neighboring congregations. In any case, they act in opposite ways when it comes to hospitality. Gaius welcomes visiting teachers. Diotrephes refuses to receive them. This may have to do with his desire "to be first." Visiting teachers would be a threat to his preeminence.

loves to be first. Personal aggrandizement was what Diotrephes craved.

v. 10 John here identifies three aspects of Diotrephes' behavior which is not in accord with the Gospel.

I will call attention. John may be forced to deal with this challenge to his apostolic authority.

gossiping maliciously. The first thing Diotrephes did was to attempt to undermine John's authority by "talking nonsense" about him—which is what this phrase means literally.

refuses to welcome. Second, he defies John's instructions and refuses to offer hospitality to Christian brothers.

puts them out of the church. Third, he is not content simply to "refuse to welcome" these missionaries, he prevents others from offering hospitality by threatening excommunication.

v. 11 *imitate.* John warns Gaius not to model his behavior after that of Diotrephes. Instead, he should copy a good example.

Anyone who does what is good is from God. Behavior is indicative of a relationship with God—or, as John goes on to say, the lack of a relationship with God.

v. 12 John names yet another first-century Christian leader: Demetrius. He gives a three-fold testimony to his character. He is well regarded by all who know him. His Christian character is self-evident. And he is highly regarded by John himself.

Demetrius. Demetrius probably delivered this letter to Gaius. Since he was unknown to Gaius, John writes this three-way recommendation. Demetrius may have been a wandering missionary whom John wishes the house-church to receive. Two other men by the name of Demetrius are mentioned in the New Testament: the silversmith in Ephesus (Acts 19:23–27) and a friend of Paul (Col. 4:14; 2 Tim. 4:10; Philem. 24—Demas is short for Demetrius). An ancient document says that John appointed the Demetrius mentioned here to be bishop of Philadelphia.

vv. 13–14 These verses are virtually identical to 2 John 12. See the notes for that verse.